T0219230

Just Spring Data Access

Madhusudhan Konda

O'REILLY®

Beijing · Cambridge · Farnham · Köln · Sebastopol · Tokyo

Just Spring Data Access
by Madhusudhan Konda

Published by O'Reilly Media, Inc., 1005 Gravenstein Highway North, Sebastopol, CA 95472.

O'Reilly books may be purchased for educational, business, or sales promotional use. Online editions are also available for most titles (*http://my.safaribooksonline.com*). For more information, contact our corporate/institutional sales department: 800-998-9938 or *corporate@oreilly.com*.

Editors: Mike Loukides and Meghan Blanchette	**Cover Designer:** Karen Montgomery
Production Editor: Iris Febres	**Interior Designer:** David Futato
Copyeditor: Gillian McGarvey	**Illustrator:** Robert Romano
Proofreader: Iris Febres	

Revision History for the First Edition:
2012-06-01   First release

See *http://oreilly.com/catalog/errata.csp?isbn=9781449328382* for release details.

ISBN: 978-1-449-32838-2

[LSI]

1339525014

Table of Contents

Foreword

Reading headlines like "Facebook moves 30-petabyte Hadoop cluster to new data center" shows that one of the biggest struggles we are facing today is Big Data and its management. Data centric applications, mobile front ends to complex data structures, and serving millions of clients accessing our datasets while handling billions of transactions a day shows that keeping data management simple and easy to handle is a first class problem in modern application development.

Thankfully, tools like Spring Data and it's many utilities make it easy to access these data sets using whichever flavor of standards best fits our team's skills and needs. While Java blazed the trail by offering the flexible but consistent JDBC standard, it was the power of Spring that cut out the tedious amounts of boilerplate afforded to us by historical SQL paradigms. This has empowered developers to focus on business logic, scaling requirements, mobile platform support, and other numerous requirements while allowing Spring to handle the chores of managing connections and interacting with various data management technologies. This is analogous to migrating from the manual memory management of coding in C to Java's sophisticated garbage collection, which removed a whole host of bugs we as developers used to face every day. By reducing the total amount of code we must write to access our own Big Data, we quickly cut out a huge number of potential bugs on Day One of our own projects.

It is refreshing to read a slim and trim book like *Just Spring Data Access*, which avoids the ever popular thick-as-possible approach and instead tries to be as clear and to-the-point as possible. For the fledgling developer that has just joined a team that uses Spring Data, this book provides a fantastic means to "catch up" over the weekend and be ready to dive in on Monday. For an architect trying to choose which standard to use for a new system, it also provides a quick read, allowing him or her to start their evaluation with something more concrete than some cobbled together opinions. Finally, for the more seasoned developer, it provides a good reference to look back and polish up skills in the arena of data management and the options provided by competing Java standards. None of us are experts on everything, and having a tightly focused book is often just what we need to hone in and solve the problems we have.

—Greg Turnquist, Senior Software Engineer at SpringSource, a division of VMware, and author of *Spring Python 1.1*

Preface

There are two different worlds: the world where none other than objects are known, and the world where data is represented in a traditional row-column format. Bringing these two worlds together is always a cumbersome task, and many times is asking for trouble. However, we have no option: they must work together!

We have JDBC to some extent, but the intricacies and complexities of persistence of Java objects to a relational databases was still a greater challenge. The Object Relational Mapping frameworks—Hibernate being the most popular open source framework—has taken away a lot of pain and grief from the developer. Spring framework has gone one more step further to simplify the usage even further.

This book in an attempt in bringing the framework closer to the developer. With simple and plain language, along with easy to understand examples, this book covers just the required bits for data access in a Java world.

This book covers JDBC, Hibernate, JPA, and JDO, as well as Spring's take on these technologies.

My goal is to deliver simple, straight-to-the-point explanations with intuitive, example-driven, engaging books! If you pick up the book, you should finish it in a day or two at most!

I sincerely believe that one will gain adequate knowledge and ammunition after reading this book.

One would require the basic understanding of Java and Spring Framework as a pre-requisite to this book. I am expecting you to enjoy this simple read. Please do get in touch even if you are unsatisfied with my writings.

If you are in London, ping me (and perhaps buy me a coffee) for a meetup. Additionally, I am easily accessible via email (madhusudhan@madhusudhan.com) or via Twitter (@mkonda007).

Conventions Used in This Book

The following typographical conventions are used in this book:

Italic

> Indicates new terms, URLs, email addresses, filenames, and file extensions.

`Constant width`

> Used for program listings, as well as within paragraphs to refer to program elements such as variable or function names, databases, data types, environment variables, statements, and keywords.

`Constant width bold`

> Shows commands or other text that should be typed literally by the user.

`Constant width italic`

> Shows text that should be replaced with user-supplied values or by values determined by context.

> This icon signifies a tip, suggestion, or general note.

> This icon indicates a warning or caution.

Using Code Examples

This book is here to help you get your job done. In general, you may use the code in this book in your programs and documentation. You do not need to contact us for permission unless you're reproducing a significant portion of the code. For example, writing a program that uses several chunks of code from this book does not require permission. Selling or distributing a CD-ROM of examples from O'Reilly books does require permission. Answering a question by citing this book and quoting example code does not require permission. Incorporating a significant amount of example code from this book into your product's documentation does require permission.

We appreciate, but do not require, attribution. An attribution usually includes the title, author, publisher, and ISBN. For example: "*Just Spring Data Access* by Madhusudhan Konda (O'Reilly). Copyright 2012 Madhusudhan Konda, 978-1-449-32838-2."

If you feel your use of code examples falls outside fair use or the permission given above, feel free to contact us at *permissions@oreilly.com*.

Safari® Books Online

Safari Books Online (*www.safaribooksonline.com*) is an on-demand digital library that delivers expert content in both book and video form from the world's leading authors in technology and business.

Technology professionals, software developers, web designers, and business and creative professionals use Safari Books Online as their primary resource for research, problem solving, learning, and certification training.

Safari Books Online offers a range of product mixes and pricing programs for organizations, government agencies, and individuals. Subscribers have access to thousands of books, training videos, and prepublication manuscripts in one fully searchable database from publishers like O'Reilly Media, Prentice Hall Professional, Addison-Wesley Professional, Microsoft Press, Sams, Que, Peachpit Press, Focal Press, Cisco Press, John Wiley & Sons, Syngress, Morgan Kaufmann, IBM Redbooks, Packt, Adobe Press, FT Press, Apress, Manning, New Riders, McGraw-Hill, Jones & Bartlett, Course Technology, and dozens more. For more information about Safari Books Online, please visit us online.

How to Contact Us

Please address comments and questions concerning this book to the publisher:

O'Reilly Media, Inc.
1005 Gravenstein Highway North
Sebastopol, CA 95472
800-998-9938 (in the United States or Canada)
707-829-0515 (international or local)
707-829-0104 (fax)

We have a web page for this book, where we list errata, examples, and any additional information. You can access this page at:

http://oreil.ly/JustSpringData

To comment or ask technical questions about this book, send email to:

bookquestions@oreilly.com

For more information about our books, courses, conferences, and news, see our website at *http://www.oreilly.com*.

Find us on Facebook: *http://facebook.com/oreilly*

Follow us on Twitter: *http://twitter.com/oreillymedia*

Watch us on YouTube: *http://www.youtube.com/oreillymedia*

Acknowledgments

I sincerely wish to thank my editors, Mike Loukides and Meghan Blanchette, and to all of those at O'Reilly, especially Iris Febres for helping shape this book.

I also sincerely express my deepest gratitude to Greg Turnquist for his guidance throughout the project.

A big thanks to goes to my family, especially to my loving wife, Jeannette, for being very patient and supportive. Also to my loving five-year-old son, Joshua, who sacrificed his free time, allowing me to write when I explained to him what I was doing in return for a trip to Disneyland!

I also thank my family in India for their wonderful support and love.

This book was written in memory of my loving Dad—we all miss you, Dad!

CHAPTER 1

Basics

Persistence of data is a challenging task for developers. There are many things that could go wrong. The introduction of JDBC has given the developer community a bit of joy by taking away painstakingly cumbersome database access in Java applications. However, there are a few wrinkles that come with JDBC, such as having to write boilerplate code, finding out a clue from the SQLExcetion stacktrace, resource management, and so on.

Spring has gone further in simplifying the data access by providing a simple and straightforward framework. This chapter discusses Spring's take on JDBC, and how Spring simplified the JDBC programming model; it did so by employing simple yet powerful mechanisms, such as Dependency Injection, Templates, and other patterns.

Using Plain JDBC

With the advent of JDBC, accessing data from a Java application has become relatively easy. Not only do we have independence from database vendor lock-in, but we also have a standard API to access multitude of databases.

However, the steps involved in using a JDBC are always the same—obtain a connection, create a Statement, execute a query, run it through ResultSet, and release the resources.

The following code demonstrates a simple example of selecting the TRADES data using plain JDBC:

```
public class JdbcPlainTest {

  private String DB_URL="jdbc:mysql://localhost:3306/JSDATA";
  private final String USER_NAME = "XXXX";
  private final String PASSWORD = "XXXX";

  private Connection createConnection() {
    Connection conn = null;
    try {
      Class.forName("com.mysql.jdbc.Driver");
      conn =
```

```
      DriverManager.getConnection(DB_URL, USER_NAME,PASSWORD);

    } catch (ClassNotFoundException e) {
      e.printStackTrace();
    } catch (SQLException e) {
      e.printStackTrace();
    }
    return conn;
  }

  private void query() {
    ResultSet rs = null;
    Statement stmt = null;
    Connection conn = createConnection();

    try {
      stmt = conn.createStatement();
      rs = stmt.executeQuery("SELECT * FROM TRADES");

      while (rs.next())
        System.out.println(rs.getString(1));
    } catch (SQLException e) {
      e.printStackTrace();
    } finally {
      try {
        rs.close();
        stmt.close();
        conn.close();
      } catch (SQLException ex) {
        e.printStackTrace();
      }
    }
  }

  public static void main(String args[]) {
    JdbcPlainTest t = new JdbcPlainTest();
    t.query();
  }
}
```

Phew! That's a lot of code for a simple task! Did you notice the code around exceptions?

There are a few things that you could have noticed from the above example:

- The resource management (creating and closing connections and statements) is a repetitious process.
- The SQLException must be caught in both the creation and destruction processes.
- The actual business logic is not more than a couple of lines; unfortunately, code is cluttered with lot of JDBC API statements and calls.

We can create a home-grown framework with callbacks and handlers to resolve these issues. Although it does work, creating your own framework leads to several issues—maintenance, extending to suit newer requirements, extensive testing, and others.

If there's already a framework that does this work, why reinvent the wheel?

The Spring data access framework is specifically created to address these problems. It is a beautiful framework that promotes *Dependency Injection* principles and carries multiple features.

Spring Data Access

The Spring data access framework has made the developer's job very easy!

It creates a rich framework in which, or from which to access databases by decoupling our code from the access mechanisms. As always, the framework heavily uses *Dependency Injection* patterns, so decoupling of our code really comes to life. The components using framework's API are easily testable, too. Moreover, there's no exceptions that we should have to catch when using the APIs!

The access logic revolves around *Template* patterns and Support classes. These patterns hide away all the boilerplate code and allows the developer to concentrate solely on business logic.

Templates

From the previous example, we can see that there is a lot of code that's not central to business function. It would be ideal to wrap up the non-critical code away from our business code in a separate class. Spring's `JdbcTemplate` class does exactly that.

This class wraps up all the access logic so users only need to concentrate on the heart of the application. If you understand the workings of `JdbcTemplate`, I would say you've conquered most of Spring's data access workings.

In addition to the standard `JdbcTemplate`, there are two other variations of the Template class: `SimpleJdbcTemplate` and `NamedParameterJdbcTemplate`. These two varieties are nothing but wrappers around `JdbcTemplate` that are used for special cases. We will discuss all of these in the coming sections. Before we work out examples, we have to carry out some prerequisites such as creating a database schema and prepopulating test data.

If you already have a database in place, you can skip this section without any concern.

MySQL Database Scripts

I am using MySQL as the database for all of the examples provided in this book. Setting up the database is easy if you follow the instructions from the provider carefully.

Once you have MySQL set up, make sure you run the SQL scripts provided by the book's source code. These scripts will create a database called `JSDATA` and create necessary tables such as `ACCOUNTS`, `TRADES`, `PRICES`, and others. If you are working with some other database, you should be able to run the scripts without any issues; personally, I have not tested them.

The next important thing is to create a `DataSource`. The `DataSource` encapsulates the database provider information and hence acts like a connection factory by fetching connections to talk to the database. It should be created by driver information such as URL, username, password, and other information. Make sure that you supply the necessary provider (driver) information to construct a `DataSource` if you are using any other databases.

The datasource-beans.xml file shown below creates a `DataSource` for MySQL database:

```
<bean id="mySqlDataSource" class="org.apache.commons.dbcp.BasicDataSource"
   destroy-method="close">
   <property name="driverClassName" value="com.mysql.jdbc.Driver" />
   <property name="url" value="jdbc:mysql://localhost:3306/JSDATA" />
   ....
</bean>
```

The class attribute points to an implementor of the `DataSource` interface; in the above snippet, it is a `BasicDataSource` class from Apache Common's DBCP project. The `driverClassName` points to a class that will be specific to a database.

We will see the full definition in a minute.

Throughout the book, we will use DBCP datasource, which can be downloaded from the site: *http://commons.apache.org/dbcp/*. If you are using Maven, add the snippet to your *pom.xml* file (check out the full *pom.xml* provided with the book's source code) to include DBCP and MySQL connector jars:

```
<!-- pom.xml -->
<dependency>
   <groupId>commons-dbcp</groupId>
   <artifactId>commons-dbcp</artifactId>
   <version>1.4</version>
</dependency>
<dependency>
   <groupId>mysql</groupId>
   <artifactId>mysql-connector-java</artifactId>
   <version>5.1.18</version>
</dependency>
```

Using JdbcTemplate

The `JdbcTemplate` is a framework class utilized for data access operations such as queries, inserts, and deletes. It is the fundamental class in the framework, so we dwell on it in detail here.

Note that the `JdbcTemplate` is a thread safe class—it can be easily shared across your threads. One of the biggest advantages in using the `JdbcTemplate` is its ability to clean up resources. Most developers forget to close the JDBC connections and other related resources, which leads to lots of issues. JdbcTemplate comes to our rescue in doing the house cleaning job for us!

Before we work with JdbcTemplate, we must set the DataSource first. This is a mandatory requirement that JdbcTemplate be configured with a DataSource object so the template will be able to create connections and statements behind the scenes.

Configuring a DataSource

As we have already seen, the javax.sql.DataSource is an interface that determines the connection details for a particular provider. Each provider will have their own implementation of the class, usually provided in a Jar file. The MySQL driver class is defined by the com.mysql.jdbc.Driver class, for example.

The following configuration shows how to set up a data source for MySQL:

```
<?xml version="1.0" encoding="UTF-8"?>
<beans xmlns="http://www.springframework.org/schema/beans"
  xmlns:xsi="http://www.w3.org/2001/XMLSchema-instance"
  xmlns:context="http://www.springframework.org/schema/context"
  xsi:schemaLocation="http://www.springframework.org/schema/beans
    http://www.springframework.org/schema/beans/spring-beans.xsd
    http://www.springframework.org/schema/context
    http://www.springframework.org/schema/context/spring-context-3.0.xsd">

  <!-- MySql DataSource -->

  <bean id="mySqlDataSource" class="org.apache.commons.dbcp.BasicDataSource">
      <property name="driverClassName" value="com.mysql.jdbc.Driver"/>
      <property name="url" value="jdbc:mysql://localhost:3306/JSDATA"/>
      <property name="username" value="jsuser"/>
      <property name="password" value="jsuser"/>
  </bean>

</beans>
```

The above snippet will create a bean named mySqlDataSource that points to a MySQL database running on localhost, directed by the url property. If we are using other providers, we need to create another bean with the same properties, but with appropriate values relevant to our provider.

Configuring JdbcTemplate

Now that the data source has been configured, the next step is to create and work with the JdbcTemplate class.

There are couple of ways to create this class. One is to create an instance in your class and provide a preconfigured data source, and the other is to create and instantiate the bean in the configuration file and inject it into your Data Access Object (DAO) classes. The DAOs are the classes that talk to databases in order to fulfill the data access functions.

Let's see an example of instantiating `JdbcTemplate` with a preconfigured `DataSource`.

```
public class JdbcTemplateTest {
  private ApplicationContext ctx = null;
  private JdbcTemplate template = null;
  private DataSource datasource = null;

  public JdbcTemplateTest() {
    // Create a container forming the beans from datasource XML file
    ctx = new ClassPathXmlApplicationContext("datasources-beans.xml");

    // DataSource bean has been fetched from the container
    datasource = ctx.getBean("mySqlDataSource",DataSource.class);

    // Instantiate the template with the datasource
    template = new JdbcTemplate(datasource);
  }

  public static void main(String[] args) {
    JdbcTemplateTest t = new JdbcTemplateTest();

    // execute the data access methods from here
    ....
  }
}
```

The steps are simple:

- Load and fetch the context from a config file that consists of datasources (in our case, it's the *datasouces-beans.xml*)
- Create the `JdbcTemplate` using the new operator providing the datasource bean to its constructor

Once you have the `JdbcTemplate` fully configured and functional, you are ready to use it to access our databast tables. The `JdbcTemplate` has a lot of functionality that requires a bit of detail study.

Working with JdbcTemplate

The `JdbcTemplate` has more than 100 methods that give varied access to data sets!

For example, you may wish to execute straight queries such as inserting data or creating tables. You can use the `execute()` method exposed on the `JdbcTemplate` for such actions.

Likewise, if you wish to query for single or multiple data rows, you should be using queryForXXX methods. There are lots of other methods, some of them are self explanatory and others are easy to follow using JavaDoc. We will cover the most important of all of these methods in the coming sections.

Querying for Single and Multiple Rows. Let's say our requirement is to find out the number of rows present in the TRADES table.

The following snippet shows the usage of JdbcTemplate in its simplest form—for fetching the number of TRADES in the table:

```
public int getTradesCount(){

    int numOfTrades =
        template.queryForInt("select count(*) from TRADES");

    return numOfTrades;
}
```

The queryForInt() method returns the count(*) equivalent from the table. The return type is obviously an integer. There are few variants of queryForXXX methods such as queryForString, queryForLong, queryForMap, and queryForObject. Basically, these are facility methods that convert your column value to an appropriate data type.

You can also rewrite the above example by using the more generic queryForObject method. However, the method takes a second parameter, which basically describes the return value's data type. In our example, because count(*) will return an integer, we pass the Integer class to the method call.

This is illustrated below:

```
public int getTradesCount(){
    int numOfTrades =
        template.queryForObject("select count(*) from TRADES",Integer.class);
    return numOfTrades;
}

// Another example of get the max id of the
// trade using queryForObject method

public int getTradeMaxId(){
    int maxId =
        template.queryForObject("select max(id) from TRADES", Integer.class);
    return maxId;
}
```

The above snippet also provides another example of using the queryForObject method to query for a Trade that has a maximum id. The queryForLong and queryForString follow the same pattern, returning a Long and String value, respectively.

The queryForMap returns a single row in a Map<String,Object> format as shown below:

```
public Map<String,Object> getTradeAsMap(){

    // note that we have hardcoded ID here!
    Map<String,Object> tradeAsMap =
        template.queryForMap("select * from TRADES where id=1");

    System.out.println("Trades Map:"+tradeAsMap);

    return tradeAsMap;
}
```

```
//The output to the console is:

Trades Map:{ID=1, ACCOUNT=1234AAA, SECURITY=MDMD,
    QUANTITY=100000, STATUS=NEW, DIRECTION=BUY}
```

As you can see, each column name is the key represented by String while the value is represented by the Object in the Map<String,Object> declaration.

However, the queryForList is a bit different to others in that it can return multiple rows. The rows are returned as a List of Map<String,Object> format.

Let's see this at work. The getAllTrades() method fetches all of the trades and prints out to the console:

```
public List<Map<String,Object>> getAllTrades(){

  List<Map<String,Object>> trades =
    template.queryForList("select * from TRADES");

  System.out.println("All Trades:"+trades);

  return trades;
}

//Prints to console as:

All Trades:
[{ID=1, ACCOUNT=1234AAA, ... STATUS=NEW, DIRECTION=BUY},
  ...,
{ID=5, ACCOUNT=452SEVE, ... STATUS=NEW, DIRECTION=SELL}]
```

The queries that we used in the above examples are fairly simple. We can also write complex queries that can be executed in the same fashion. We often use where clauses and other SQL constructs to execute complex queries. However, the where clause requires input variables to be set. How can we parameterize these bind variables?

Bind Variables. Bind variables help to create a dynamic SQL query. If our requirement is to fetch records based on various conditions, we usually use the where clause in our SQL script. Bind variables are the preferred option as opposed to using inline variables because they protect our application against SQL injection attacks.

For example, if we have to get the STATUS of a Trade whose id is 5, we need to write the SQL as follows:

```
public String getTradeStatus(int id){

  String status =
    template.queryForObject("select STATUS from TRADES where id= ?",
    new Object[]{id}, String.class);

  return status;
}
```

The ? will be an indication to the framework to substitute the value with the second parameter of the method, which in the above case is the id. The way to do this is to create an array of Object with your incoming id value. The third parameter is the type of value the method query is expected to return; in this case, the STATUS is a String type.

We can provide more than a one bind variable, no restriction on the number.

In the following snippet, the overloaded getTradeStatus() method has two conditions in the where clause and accordingly, we provide a second value via a second parameter, Object array:

```
public String getTradeStatus(int id, String security){

  String status =
    template.queryForObject("select STATUS from TRADES where id = ? and security=?",
    new Object[]{id,security}, String.class);

  return status;
}
```

Mapping Rows to Domain Objects. We know that each row in the TRADES table is represented by our Trade domain object. Although we have seen fetching the Trades from the table, we have not yet seen how we create a Trade object from each row of the record.

In order to do this, we need to use a RowMapper callback provided by the framework. The RowMapper interface has one method—mapRow—where you need to map the incoming row to the domain object. You can create the RowMapper as an anonymous class or you can have your own class implementing the RowMapper interface separately.

Let's take a look at each one separately.

First, we create a TradeMapper class that implements the RowMapper interface and defines its single method:

```
private static final class TradeMapper implements RowMapper<Trade>{
  @Override
  public Trade mapRow(ResultSet rs, int rowNum) throws SQLException {
    Trade t = new Trade();
    // set the values by use ResultSet's getXXX methods
    t.setId(rs.getInt("ID"));
    ....

    return t;
  }
}
```

In the mapRow method, a ResultSet instance for the current row is given to us via this callback. What we are doing is extracting the column data from the ResultSet object and setting the values against our newly instantiated domain object Trade. The method then retuns the fully initialized Trade object.

As we now have our RowMapper implementation ready, we give it to the overloaded queryForObject method to retrieve all the trades from the table:

```
public Trade getMappedTrade(int id){

    Trade trade = template.queryForObject("select * from TRADES where id = ?",
      new Object[]{id} ,
      new TradeMapper());

    return trade;

}
```

Did you notice the third argument to the method? It's taking our TradeMapper class, which creates the Trade with the column values extracted from the ResultSet. The good thing about this callback class is that we can use it anywhere that a method expects a RowMapper to convert the column data to Trade object.

There's an alternative way of using RowMapper—we can also use an anonymous class to create a RowMapper instead of creating a separate instance as we have seen above. The way to do so is illustrated below:

```
public Trade getTrade(int id){
    Trade trade = template.queryForObject("select * from TRADES where id= ?",
    new Object[]{id},
    new RowMapper<Trade>(){
      @Override
      public Trade mapRow(ResultSet rs, int row) throws SQLException {
        Trade t = new Trade();
        t.setId(rs.getInt("ID"));
        t.setAccount(rs.getString("ACCOUNT"));
        ....
        t.setDirection(rs.getString("DIRECTION"));
      return t;
      }
  });
    return trade;
  }
```

The RowMapper that is instantiated inline as an anonymous class does exactly the same thing that we saw earlier.

Note that second argument in the mapRow corresponds to the row number of the record given to the callback. Also, keep in mind that the ResultSet given to your callback has only one record. Any use of ResultSet.next() will throw a SQLException.

Creating the RowMapper class anonymously has a limited scope—it can't be used anywhere else in the application. Unless you have a strong case to use the anonymous class, go with a separate class like TradeMapper and reuse it. Reusability scores good marks!

Note that both the JdbcTemplate and RowMapper classes are thread safe. You can share them and use them across threads without having to worry about state corruption.

Fetching List of Trades. Now that we know how to fetch a single record and map to a domain object, let's see how to get the list of all rows mapped to domain objects. Actually, it is quite straight forward now that you have a RowMapper class already designed.

The following snippet is used to fetch such a list. Note that the only change was using query() method rather than queryForXXX method:

```
public List<Trade> getAllMappedTrades(){

    List<Trade> trades =
      template.query("select * from TRADES", new TradeMapper());

    return trades;
}
```

For each row fetched, a respective Trade object will be formed by the TradeMapper and then added to the list—simple!

Now that you've seen various query mechanisms, let's look at the update and delete workings, too.

Inserting, Deleting, and Updating Rows

We also use the JdbcTemplate to do the updates. We use JdbcTemplate.update() variants to execute the appropriate statements. The following snippet shows inserting a Trade into TRADES table:

```
private void insertTrade() {

    int rowsUpdated =
      template.update("insert into TRADES values(?,?,?,?,?,?)",
        61,"JSDATA","REV",500000,"NEW","SELL");

    System.out.println("Rows Updated:"+rowsUpdated);
}
```

The return value indicates the rows affected. Note that we use bind variables in the above query.

Similarly, use the same update method to update the values of the rows. The following example shows how to update the status of an existing Trade:

```
private void updateTrade(String status, int id) {

    int rowsUpdated =
      template.update("update TRADES set status='"+status+"' where id="+id+"");

    System.out.println("Rows Updated:"+rowsUpdated);
}
```

The above statement looks a little bit ugly with all the String concatenation. Is there any other way of doing this job?

There is a way. You can use the another variant of the update method that takes varargs:

```
private void updateTrade(String status, int id) {
    int rowsUpdated =
      template.update("update TRADES set status=? where id=?",status, id);
```

```
  System.out.println("Rows Updated:"+rowsUpdated);
}
```

There's another overloaded method that sets the bind variables using an `Object` array (which we have already seen in our query examples earlier) and `java.sql.Types` array. The types array will provide the necessary framework tools to typecast the variables.

In the following `updateTradeUsingTypes` method, we are using the types array to let the framework know the bind values type. However, as the `status` and `id` are already known types, perhaps using the types array might not be needed except for the compiler's sake.

```
private void updateTradeUsingTypes(String status, int id) {

  int rowsUpdated = template.update(
    "update TRADES set status=? where id=?",
    new Object[] { status, id },
    new int[] { java.sql.Types.VARCHAR, java.sql.Types.INTEGER });

  System.out.println("Rows Updated:" + rowsUpdated);
}
```

However, see the updated snippet below where using SQL types comes necessary—we pass in all the arguments as `String` objects.

```
private void updateTradeUsingTypes() {

  int rowsUpdated = template.update(
    "update TRADES set status=? where id=?",
    new Object[] { "UNKNOWN","6" },
    new int[] { java.sql.Types.VARCHAR,java.sql.Types.INTEGER });

  System.out.println("Rows Updated:" + rowsUpdated);
}
```

You can also invoke a *Stored Procedure* using the `update` method, as shown here:

```
private void replayTradesUsingSP(List tradeIds) {

  template.update(
    "call JSDATA.REPLAY_TRADES_SP (?)", tradeIds);
}
```

The `REPLAY_TRADES_SP` stored procedure picks up all the `trades` identified by the `trade Ids` list and replay them.

Executing Statements

The `JdbcTemplate` exposes `execute` methods so you can run `Data Definition Language` (DDL) statements easily:

```
public void createAndDropPersonTable(){
  template.execute("create table PERSON
    (FIRST_NAME varchar(50) not null, LAST_NAME varchar(50) not null)");

  // drop the table
  template.execute("drop table PERSON");
```

```
    System.out.println("Table dropped");
}
```

Summary

In this chapter, we began the problem statement by discussing the wrinkles around Java database programming using standard JDBC APIs. We identified the boiler plate code around the usage in relation to the resource management and jumped to see what Spring's framework has done to address them. The Spring's framework has wrapped up the unnecessary boilerplate code into templates. We have seen the fundamental class of the framework—JdbcTemplate—in action. We learned how to utilize the class using simple examples.

The next chapter will discuss the additional templates along with advanced Spring JDBC usage using Support classes and callbacks.

CHAPTER 2

Advanced Concepts

The Spring framework has provided extensive APIs to work with the database. We've covered the basics of the framework in the last chapter, especially using the versatile `JdbcTemplate` class. This chapter elaborates on advanced concepts, including other templates, callbacks, and batch operations.

NamedParameterJdbcTemplate

In our queries, we define the bind variables using a ? operator as shown in the following snippet:

```
select count(*) from TRADES
  where account = ? and security = ?
```

If we have a handful of these parameters, it would be an eyesore to read a query with ? all over the place. Spring has defined a new `NamedParameterJdbcTemplate` class that comes handy in eliminating these placeholder variables. This class basically encapsulates the `JdbcTemplate` by providing the enhanced functionality of declaring the bind variables using named parameters.

The same query can be tweaked as shown below using appropriate names instead of ? variables:

```
select count(*) from TRADES
  where account = :account and security = :security
```

The `:account` and `:security` names indicate that these variables will be passed in by some means. Note the colon (:) before the variable; this is the syntax you must follow.

There are two ways of setting these variables. One is to use a simple `Map` with the variables as the keys, and the other is to use `SqlParameterSource`, a utility provided by the framework.

Using Map

The following snippet shows how to set the variables by using a map with keys:

```
public int getTradesCount(String s, String a){
  Map bindValues = new HashMap();
  bindValues.put("status", s);
  bindValues.put("account", a);
  int numOfTrades = template.queryForInt
    ("select count(*) from TRADES where account=:account and status=:status",
bindValues);
  System.out.println("Number of Trades: "+numOfTrades);
  return numOfTrades;
}
```

In the above example, we populate the Map with the provided arguments setting them to the status and account keys. Then we pass this Map to the query. Did you notice the names in the query? The names declared in the query must match the keys of our Map.

Using SqlParameterSource

The second way of setting the bind variables is by using framework's helper interface, SqlParameterSource. There's an out-of-box implementation available in the form of MapSqlParameterSource which acts as a wrapper around Map. The way to set values is to use the addValue() method and chain them as shown below:

```
public int getTradesCountUsingSqlParameterSource(String s, String a){
  SqlParameterSource bindValues =
    new MapSqlParameterSource().addValue("status", s).addValue("account", a);
  int numOfTrades = template.queryForInt
    ("select count(*) from TRADES
      where account=:account and status=:status", bindValues);
  ...
}
```

There is another implementation of the same interface which works on extracting the values from a Java object that complies to JavaBean standards. The BeanPropertySql ParameterSource takes an instance and finds the values of the properties. See the following example to understand the usage:

```
public int getTradesCountUsingBeanSqlParameterSource(Trade t){
  SqlParameterSource bindValues = new BeanPropertySqlParameterSource(t);
  int numOfTrades = template.queryForInt
    ("select count(*) from TRADES where account=:account and status=:status",
bindValues);
}
```

The class browses through the Trade object to find the respective properties—in our case, status and account. The following snippet shows the way to call the method. The query will use the account 1234AAAA and status NEW as the arguments retrieved from the Trade bean.

```
public static void main(String[] args) {
  NamedParameterJdbcTemplateTest t = new NamedParameterJdbcTemplateTest();

  Trade trade = new Trade();
  trade.setAccount("1234AAA");
  trade.setId(1234);
  trade.setStatus("NEW");

  int count = t.getTradesCountUsingBeanSqlParameterSource(trade);
}
```

As the name suggests, the NamedParameterJdbcTemplate is used primarily for replacing the '?' property placeholders with appropriate human readable names. Should you need to use the JdbcTemplate for any reason, use the getJdbcOperations() exposed on the NamedParameterJdbcTemplate class. This will let you have access to all the methods exposed via JdbcTemplate class.

Jdbc Batching

Executing lots of updates or inserts *one after another* is a cumbersome operation. If your JDBC Driver supports, batching is an excellent strategy for improving performance. For example, if you wish to insert 10,000 trades, you can insert them in a batch size of 100, 500, 1,000, or any other number. The JDBC statement will be re-used when executing the batch instead of creating new statements every time you execute a call to a database operation. Another advantage is that the round trips to the database (usually over the network) are drastically reduced.

Both JdbcTemplate and NamedParameterJdbcTemplate provide support for batch executions. Again, there are couple of ways of doing this: using the framework's utility class SqlParameterSourceUtils or extending the framework's BatchPreparedStatementSetter interface.

Using SqlParameterSourceUtils

The SqlParameterSourceUtils is a handy utility class the converts the List to an array of SqlParameterSource instances.

The snippet shown below shows how we use it in action:

```
private int[] insertTradesList(final List<Trade> trades) {
  SqlParameterSource[] tradesList =
    SqlParameterSourceUtils.createBatch(trades.toArray());

  int[] updatesCount = namedTemplate.batchUpdate(
    "insert into TRADES values
      (:id,:account,:security,:quantity,:status,:direction)",
    tradesList);
  return updatesCount;
}
```

You pass in a List of `Trade`s that will be converted to an array of `SqlParameterSource` by the `SqlParameterSourceUtils` utility class. This array is then passed to our template for execution, which returns the rows that were inserted into database.

Using BatchPreparedStatementSetter

Alternatively, you could implement the framework's batch interface `BatchPre paredStatementSetter` and use it. You should set the values on the `PreparedStatement` by implementing the `BatchPreparedStatementSetter` interface's `setValues()` method. Set the batch size by implementing another method `getBatchSize()` as shown below:

```
private int[] insertTrades(final List<Trade> trades) {
  int[] updatesCount = template.batchUpdate(
    "insert into TRADES values(?,?,?,?,?,?)",
    new BatchPreparedStatementSetter() {
    @Override
    public void setValues(PreparedStatement ps, int i) throws SQLException {
      Trade t = trades.get(i);
      ps.setInt(1, t.getId());
      ...
    }

    @Override
    public int getBatchSize() {
      return 10;
    }
  });

  return updatesCount;
}
```

In the above example, the `setValues()` method will be invoked ten times. This method is similar to the one used for `getBatchSize()`, which utilizes the same `PreparedStatement` for all the calls. This is an improvement.

How would you go about updating larger bucket of **trades**, such as 100,000 of them? Instead of using the above strategy of calling the **insertTrades** with different batch sizes, Spring provides you with another version of the **batchUpdate** method. In this instance, it takes a batch size—say you wish to batch those hundred thousand **trades** into a batch of 1,000—which is passed in to the method as a second parameter. The addition is a `ParameterizedPreparedStatementSetter` class that implements the `setValues()` method setting values from each `Trade` on the `PreparedStatement`.

Here is an example:

```
private int[][] insertTradesInBatches(final List<Trade> trades, int batchSize){
  int[][] updateCount = template.batchUpdate(
    "insert into TRADES values(?,?,?,?,?,?)",
    trades,
    batchSize,
    new ParameterizedPreparedStatementSetter<Trade>(){
    @Override
```

```
    public void setValues(PreparedStatement ps, Trade t) throws SQLException {
      ps.setInt(1, t.getId());
      ...
    }});
  return updateCount;
}
```

The returned two dimensional integer array indicates the number of batches against updates in each batch.

Simple JDBC Classes

If I tell you that you can operate inserts on the tables without writing any SQL statements, what would be your reaction? I think you would jump for joy, don't you?

The framework provides a couple of utility classes that work intelligently without us having to write SQL statements. The `SimpleJdbcInsert` and `SimpleJdbcCall` classes are designed to take advantage of the metadata returned by the JDBC driver. They understand the column names, types, and other relevant information.

Let's see them at work.

SimpleJDBCInsert Class

The `SimpleJDBCInsert` class is used to execute inserts with minimalistic configuration.

The first thing you need to do is to instantiate the class with a `DataSource` and set the table name by invoking the method `withTableName()`.

The following example shows this:

```
private SimpleJdbcInsert jdbcInsert = null;

// Get the datasource
datasource = ctx.getBean("mySqlDataSource", DataSource.class);

//Create the instance associating with the table
jdbcInsert = new SimpleJdbcInsert(datasource).withTableName("TRADES");
```

Now that the object is ready, we invoke the `execute()` method that takes a `Trade`. The values of the `trade` are set against the key values of a Map and passed to the `SimpleJdbcInsert` class:

```
public void insertTrade(Trade t) {
  Map tradeMap = new HashMap();
  tradeMap.put("id", t.getId());
  tradeMap.put("account", t.getAccount());
  ...

  jdbcInsert.execute(tradeMap);
}
```

Make sure the keys match the column names. That's it—no SQL statements and no more placeholders!

Should you wish to insert only one or two columns, you can set the column names using the usingColumns() method as shown below:

```
jdbcInsert =
  new SimpleJdbcInsert(datasource)
  .withTableName("TRADES")
  .usingColumns("id","account","security","quantity");
```

To simplify things further, instead of using Map to set the values, you can use one of the SqlParameterSource implementations.

The BeanPropertySqlParameterSource will work on the Trade object to extract the values and pass it on to the PreparedStatement. We have seen an example of this class's usage earlier in the chapter.

The following snippet summarizes it in this context:

```
public void insertTradeUsingSqlParameterSource(Trade t) {

    // create an instance passing our Trade object
    SqlParameterSource source = new BeanPropertySqlParameterSource(t);

    // all you do is to invoke execute!
    jdbcInsert.execute(source);
}
```

SimpleJdbcCall Class

Similar to the SimpleJdbcInsert class, if you want to call a Stored Procedure using minimal configuration then SimpleJdbcCall is the one that comes handy.

The trade_by_quantity is a Stored Procedure that fetches a big trade whose quantity is provided by the client. It takes the quantity as IN parameter and spits out ID and ACCOUNT values of the row as OUT parameters for the matching big trade.

```
CREATE PROCEDURE trade_by_quantity
  (IN in_qty INTEGER, OUT big_trade_id INTEGER)
  BEGIN
    SELECT id
    INTO big_trade_id
    FROM TRADES where quantity = in_qty;
  END;
```

We have a Stored Procedure created, so let's create the SimpleJdbcCall class. We instantiate the SimpleJdbcCall class by providing a data source and associating it with the Stored Procedure, as shown here below.

```
jdbcCall = new SimpleJdbcCall(datasource)
  .withProcedureName("trade_by_quantity");
```

Now that we have our class configured, we need to work on the method that invokes this class.

The method shown below does exactly that: it creates an instance of `SqlParameter Source` with quantity as the bind value and invokes the execute method on the class.

```
public Trade getBigTradeUsingSimpleJdbcCall(String quantity){

  SqlParameterSource inValues =
    new MapSqlParameterSource().addValue("quantity", quantity);

  Map bigTrades = jdbcCall.execute(inValues);
  Trade t = new Trade();
  t.setId((Integer)bigTrades.get("id"));
  t.setAccount((String)bigTrades.get("account"));

  return t;
}
```

The execute method returns a Map with the declared `OUT` parameters as the keys. What we do is to fetch them from the map based on the `OUT` parameters and set them on to the `Trade` object.

The above program returns only one `Trade`. You can also use `SimpleJdbcCall` to invoke a `StoredProc` that returns a `ResultSet`. Create the class as shown below, passing a `RowMapper` implementation—`ParameterizedBeanPropertyRowMapper` in this case.

```
jdbcCall = new SimpleJdbcCall(datasource)
  .withProcedureName("big_trades")
  .returningResultSet("trades", new ParameterizedBeanPropertyRowMapper());

Map bigTrades = jdbcCall.execute();

return (List)bigTrades.get("trades");
```

The above snippets fetches the List of `Trades` from the Map using the key `"trades"` set during the instantiation of the `SimpleJdbcCall`.

In-Memory Databases

In-memory databases such as Derby and HSQL enable speedy application development. Spring framework provides good support to use them in your applications.

Java SE comes with an in-memory database called Java DB. While Java DB is similar to Derby, it carries a fundamental difference: Oracle (Java provider) supports and maintains the Java DB while Derby is maintained outside the Java ecosystem by Apache group.

The inner workings of these databases are similar to the Relational Database Management Systems (RDBMS) that we know. We can see how Spring helps us in developing access to Java DB.

The first thing we need to do is to create a `DataSource`. It follows the same lines to normal `DataSource` definitions—make sure you provide the right driver class and URLs. Take the following, for example:

```
<bean id="javaDBDataSource"
  class="org.springframework.jdbc.datasource.DriverManagerDataSource">
  <property name="driverClassName" value="org.apache.derby.jdbc.EmbeddedDriver" />
  <property name="url"
    value="jdbc:derby:/Users/mkonda/dev/ws/JSDATA;create=true" />
  <property name="username" value="" />
  <property name="password" value="" />
</bean>
```

As we see in the above snippet, defining an in-memory `DataSource` is no different to other types of RDBMS `DataSources`. The `url` points to the local file system path where the database will be created. The appending `create=true` string at the end of the `url` indicates if the database (in this case `JSDATA`) should be created if it does not exist. Ideally, the first time you start your Java DB, leave this as true (and turn it to false later on or else the driver throws warnings!) so the schema will be created for us.

The next step is to create our `JdbcTemplate` using this injected `DataSource` as we have already seen in many earlier cases. The following snippet shows this test scenario:

```
public class JavaDBTest {
  private ApplicationContext ctx = null;
  private JdbcTemplate template = null;
  private DataSource datasource = null;

  public JavaDBTest() {
    ctx = new ClassPathXmlApplicationContext("java-db-beans.xml");

    datasource = ctx.getBean("javaDBDataSource", DataSource.class);

    // Create our template using JavaDB DataSource
    template = new JdbcTemplate(datasource);
  }

  //Insert a trade
  private void insertTrade() {
    int rowsUpdated = template.update(

      "insert into TRADES values(?,?,?,?,?,?)", 33, "JSDATA", "REV",500000, "NEW",
"SELL");

    System.out.println("Rows Updated:" + rowsUpdated);
  }

  public static void main(String[] args) {
    JavaDBTest test = new JavaDBTest();
    test.insertTrade();
  }
}
```

In-memory databases are quite useful in development mode; it really gears up the productivity to a certain degree. We do not have to change our SQL scripts when we release our code to production; only the DataSource definition needs to be changed. Additionally, it will not point to a production-RDBMS.

Callbacks

As you may have already noticed, there are two parts in any JDBC client program: one part gets the connection, creates the statement, and deals with resource management, which is more or less a boilerplate code. The other part is the heart of the application where we code the business logic.

The framework hides away the nonbusiness code efficiently in the templates while allowing us to concentrate on the business logic. It does this by providing valuable callbacks where we can deal with writing the business logic.

We have already seen a RowMapper callback in action earlier. Let's see the rest of them, such as RowCallbackHandler, PreparedStatementCallback, and CallableStatementCall back here.

PreparedStatement Callback

Should you have a requirement to run the code in your own PreparedStatement, rely on this callback.

The framework will ideally create one and hands over to you via the callback.

There are two ways to get the handle to the PreparedStatement: one is by creating your own implementation class and the other is by creating an anonymous class.

Let's say we need to extract a Map of Trade id and Trade account from our TRADES table using the PreparedStatement route. To do this, we must create a class and implement the framework's PreparedStatementCallback interface to override the doInPrepared Statement method.

The following is the code snippet for the callback that executes the query in a given PrepatedStatement, which results in a ResultSet object. The Id and Account column values are extracted from the resultSet into the Map object.

```
private class PSCallback implements
PreparedStatementCallback<Map<Integer, Object>> {
  Map<Integer, Object> tradeIdAccountsMap =
new HashMap<Integer, Object>();

  @Override
  public Map<Integer, Object> doInPreparedStatement(PreparedStatement ps)
    throws SQLException, DataAccessException {

    ResultSet rs = ps.executeQuery();
    while (rs.next()) {
```

```
        int tradeId = rs.getInt(1);
        String account = rs.getString(2);
        tradeIdAccountsMap.put(tradeId, account);
      }
   return tradeIdAccountsMap;
  }
}
```

The actual call that instantiates this callback is given below. When the framework runs the execute method, a PreparedStatement object is created with the given SQL query and passed on to the PSCallback, object which was shown above.

```
public void getTradesMapViaPSCallback() throws Exception {

  Map<Integer, Object> tradeIdAccountsMap =
    template.execute("select * from TRADES", new PSCallback());
  System.out.println("ID-ACCOUNTS map:" + tradeIdAccountsMap);
}
```

Alternatively, you can also declare your callback inline:

```
public void getTradePSCallbackAsAnonymous() throws Exception {
  Trade t = template.execute("select * from TRADES where id=1",
    new PreparedStatementCallback<Trade>() {
      private Trade t = new Trade();
        @Override
        public Trade doInPreparedStatement(PreparedStatement ps)
          throws SQLException, DataAccessException {

          ResultSet rs = ps.executeQuery();
          while (rs.next()) {
            ...
          }
        return t;
      }
    });
  System.out.println("Trade via anonymous PS: "+t);
}
```

As you can see, we extracted one Trade from the ResultSet and returned it.

I mentioned earlier that the PreparedStatement that was given to our implementors were already pre-configured with a SQL statement.

What if we wish to create the SQL query somewhere else? It turns out that Spring has thought of this and hence provides PreparedStatementCreator interface. This means the implementation will create a statement from the connection provided.

The following snippet is the implementor of this interface. The example shows that we were given a Connection object to create a PreparedStatement using the SQL query.

```
class PSCreator implements PreparedStatementCreator {
  @Override
  public PreparedStatement createPreparedStatement(Connection con)
    throws SQLException {
```

```
        PreparedStatement ps = con
          .prepareStatement("select * from TRADES where id=?");

        ps.setLong(1, 5);
        return ps;
      }
    }
```

Use this class in your method as shown below (you can reuse your PreparedStatement
Callback implementation here):

```
public void testPSCallbackViaCreator() throws Exception {

  // Provide the creator and callback
  Map<Integer, Object> tradeIdAccountsMap =
    template.execute(new PSCreator(), new PSCallback());

  System.out.println("ID-ACCOUNTS map:" + tradeIdAccountsMap);
}
```

Callable Statement Callbacks

The framework provides a couple of callbacks for CallableStatements: the CallableS
tatementCallback and CallableStatementCreator classes.

Fortunately, they follow exactly the same footsteps as PreparedStatementXXX. For example, you have to implement CallableStatementCallback to define the doInCalla
bleStatement method, wherein you would be given CallableStatement instead:

```
public void testCSCallbackViaCreator() throws Exception {
  Map<Integer, Object> tradeIdAccountsMap = template.execute(
    "select * from TRADES", new CSCallback());
  System.out.println("ID-ACCOUNTS map:" + tradeIdAccountsMap);
}

private class CSCallback implements CallableStatementCallback {

  @Override
  public Object doInCallableStatement(CallableStatement ps)
    throws SQLException, DataAccessException {
    ResultSet rs = ps.executeQuery();
    while (rs.next()) {
      //...
    }
    return ...;
  }
}
```

You can also create an instance of CallableStatementCreator and pass it to the
execute method:

```
class CSCreator implements CallableStatementCreator {
  @Override
  public CallableStatement createCallableStatement(Connection con)
    throws SQLException {
```

```
        return null;
    }
}
```

Row Callbacks

There are couple of callbacks to handle the query results—RowCallbackHandler and ResultSetExtractor. The RowCallbackHandler is used to process the ResultSet per row.

For example, if we wish to find out the count of big trades (trades whose quantity is greater than one million) the easy way to achieve this is to implement RowCallbackHandler and define the logic in the processRow method.

The following snippet shows this:

```
class BigTradeCounter implements RowCallbackHandler {
    int bigTradeCount = 0;
    double quantity = 0;

    BigTradeCounter(double quantity) {
        this.quantity = quantity;
    }

    @Override
    public void processRow(ResultSet rs) throws SQLException {
        while (rs.next()) {
        if (rs.getDouble(4) > this.quantity) {
            System.out.println("Big Trade Id:" + rs.getString(1));
            bigTradeCount++;
        }
      }
    }
    public int getBigTradeCount() {
        return bigTradeCount;
    }
}
```

The above code checks the quantity (the rs.getDouble(4) operator will return the quantity of the Trade) to see if it's a big trade and store it in a local variable.

The following code shows the invocation:

```
private void bigTradeCountHanlder(double quantity) {
    BigTradeCounter counter = new BigTradeCounter(quantity);
    template.query("select * from TRADES", counter);
    System.out.println("Big Trades" + counter.getBigTradeCount());
}
```

You can also define the same class as an anonymous inline class.

Note that the RowMapper class that we learned about in the first chapter does the same thing. The RowCallbackHandler implementation holds onto state and hence can't be reused unless a new instance is created.

There's another framework class called RowCountCallbackHandler, which is an implementation of RowCallbackHandler. You can use this to get different attributes of the tables, such as row and column counts, column types, and others.

A usage example is shown below:

```
private void tradeCount() {
  RowCountCallbackHandler counter = new RowCountCallbackHandler();
  template.query("select * from TRADES", counter);
  System.out.println("Number of trades: " + counter.getRowCount());
}
```

Summary

In this chapter, we discussed advanced concepts supported by Spring for database programming using standard JDBC. We looked at NamedParameterJdbcTemplate which eliminates the '?' placeholders when constructing the SQL queries. We discussed Spring's support for batching. We then looked at SimpleJDBC classes that would come in handy should we wish to get rid of SQL queries altogether. We moved on to work with a few examples of in-memory databases and callbacks.

In the next chapters, we discuss Spring's support for Object Relational Mapping (ORM) tools such as Hibernate, JPA, and JDO.

CHAPTER 3

Hibernate

As Java developers, we always enjoy working with objects. We thoroughly know how to manipulate, massage, or manage objects in a Java application. However, when it comes to persisting these objects to a relational database, we get slightly uneasy. There is a reason for this—you cannot persist the objects without having to format them in a shape that the database can understand and accept. The most common way is to use some SQL in your code and request the JDBC driver to do the job of persistence on our behalf.

How easy would it be if I could save the object by simply calling a save method instead of writing JDBC code? Likewise, if we wanted to delete a row, is it not convenient to just call upon delete for an object?

We can certainly do this by employing Object Relational Mapping (ORM) tools. These tools' main job is to transform the Java objects to relational data and vice versa. There are quite a few ORMs available. One that has gained a serious following is Hibernate. Hibernate is an ORM framework that lets you work on Java objects without having to worry about SQL queries, database connections, datasources, and resource management issues. While certainly you can use Hibernate on its own in an application, using it via Spring may bring more advantages such as dependency injection and testability. This chapter looks into Spring's Hibernate offering in the ORM space while future chapters will discuss others such as iBatis.

Two-Minute Hibernate

Over the years, Hibernate has grown tremendously from pillar to post, winning the hearts of the Java developer community. It is the most sought-after framework in the Java community. Before we go into details about how Spring's framework is used to persist data via Hibernate, let's take a quick look at Hibernate from a high ground.

Hibernate is a framework that takes the burden of object persistence in a relational database. With a bit of configuration, developers can concentrate on the object for data persistence while Hibernate takes care of the object-relational mismatch problem. There are three steps involved in using Hibernate:

- Configuring the Session Factory and datasources
- Setting the Hibernate properties
- Creating the POJO and relevant mappings

Let's say our primary requirement is to persist Trades to the database. As we have seen in the earlier chapters, Trade is simply a POJO with few accessor methods. We also know that there is a corresponding table—TRADES—in our database. Our program should persist the Trade using plain Hibernate API. We will show how we can do this.

First, Hibernate requires a configuration file, called *hibernate.properties*, from where it can create a Session Factory. The following is the file located in the classpath:

```
hibernate.dialect org.hibernate.dialect.MySQL5Dialect
hibernate.connection.driver_class com.mysql.jdbc.Driver
hibernate.connection.url jdbc:mysql://localhost:3306/JSDATA
hibernate.connection.username user
hibernate.connection.password password
hibernate.current_session_context_class thread
hibernate.show_sql false
```

If you examine the property file carefully, you can observe that these are the details required to define a DataSource. Hibernate's SessionFactory also requires a datasource in order to create a connection. In the above file, we define the driver, URL, and other relevant details.

Note that you can define the same properties using a XML file, usually called as *hibernate.cfg.xml*.

The next step is to create a mapping file that maps the Trade POJO to the TRADES table columns. The following snippet shows the simple mapping:

```
<?xml version="1.0"?>
<!DOCTYPE hibernate-mapping PUBLIC
    "-//Hibernate/Hibernate Mapping DTD//EN"
    "http://hibernate.sourceforge.net/hibernate-mapping-3.0.dtd">

<hibernate-mapping>
  <class name="com.madhusudhan.jsd.domain.Trade" table="TRADES">
    <id name="id" column="ID">
      <generator class="assigned" />
    </id>
    <property name="account" column="ACCOUNT" />
    <property name="security" column="SECURITY" />
    <property name="direction" column="DIRECTION" />
    <property name="status" column="STATUS" />
    <property name="quantity" column="QUANTITY" />
  </class>
</hibernate-mapping>
```

The class attribute declares a fully qualified name of the Java object while table attribute points to the corresponding TRADES table. The id represents the key to the entity. This id can be set by employing various strategies. In the above, it was set using an application generated id's. The rest of the property tags define the mappings for other attributes. For example, the account variable of the Trade POJO will be mapped to ACCOUNTcolumn on the table.

Now that our configuration and mapping is done, it is time to write a simple client:

```
public class PlainHibernateTest {
  private SessionFactory factory = null;
  private Configuration configuration = null;
  public PlainHibernateTest() {
    configuration = new Configuration();
    configuration.addFile("Trade.hbm.xml");
    factory = configuration.buildSessionFactory();
  }

  private void testInsert(Trade t) {
    Session session = factory.getCurrentSession();
    session.beginTransaction();
    session.save(t);
    session.getTransaction().commit();
    System.out.println("Inserted Trade"+t.getId());
  }

  public static void main(String[] args) {
    Trade t = DomainUtil.createDummyTrade();
    PlainHibernateTest test = new PlainHibernateTest();
    test.testInsert(t);
  }
}
```

As you can see above, the Configuration object is created first. Behind the scenes, the framework reads the *hibernate.properties*, file which is available in the classpath and creates the Configuration object. You can provide the respective mapping files by invoking the appropriate method toward the configuration. The Configuration object is then used to create a SessionFactory.

Once you have a SessionFactory, create a Session from it and start your work. The Trade is persisted into the database when you call save() on a session. Simple, isn't it?

Using Spring Hibernate

Now that you've seen Hibernate from a high ground, let's see what Spring brings to the table.

Earlier versions of Spring used to employ a Template pattern for Hibernate specifics. However, since version 3.x, Spring folks advocate using plain Hibernate APIs via Spring's framework. We will see both of them in action.

Before we start working with the API, there is a bit of setup involved. Let's examine at this initial setup before we move on to using the Hibernate API.

Basic Setup

As we already know, the Hibernate's SessionFactory is the key class that must be created before start working with Hibernate. Spring can create this SessionFactory using it's own implementation class called LocalSessionFactoryBean. The LocalSessionFactoryBean is declared in the XML file so that the framework can create and inject the bean it into your data access classes. The configuration allows us to set Hibernate properties such as mapping files, dialects, and others.

The LocalSessionFactoryBean has to be wired in with a DataSource reference and hibernate properties.

See the configuration snippet below:

```
<bean id="sessionFactory"
  class="org.springframework.orm.hibernate3.LocalSessionFactoryBean">
  <property name="dataSource" ref="mySqlDataSource" />
  <property name="mappingResources">
    <list>
      <value>Trade.hbm.xml</value>
    </list>
  </property>

  <property name="hibernateProperties">
    <props>
      <prop key="hibernate.show_sql">false</prop>
      <prop key="hibernate.current_session_context_class">thread</prop>
      <prop key="hibernate.dialect">org.hibernate.dialect.MySQL5Dialect</prop>
      <prop key="hibernate.hbm2ddl.auto">true</prop>
    </props>
  </property>
</bean>

<bean id="mySqlDataSource" class="org.apache.commons.dbcp.BasicDataSource"
  destroy-method="close">
  ...
</bean>
```

Now that your SessionFactory has been declared, the next job is to inject this into your DAO using Spring's dependency injection mechanism. In order to do this, create a TradeDAO with a SessionFactory parameter, as shown below:

```
public class TradeDAO {
  private SessionFactory sessionFactory = null;
  private Session session = null;

  public void setSessionFactory(SessionFactory sessionFactory) {
    this.sessionFactory = sessionFactory;
  }
```

```
    public SessionFactory getSessionFactory() {
      return sessionFactory;
    }
    ...
  }
```

You must wire the SessionFactory into your TradeDAO object as declared in the XML config below:

```
<bean id="tradeDAO" class="com.madhusudhan.jsd.hibernate.TradeDAO">
  <property name="sessionFactory" ref="sessionFactory"/>
</bean>

<bean id="sessionFactory"
  class="org.springframework.orm.hibernate3.LocalSessionFactoryBean">
  ...
</bean>
```

That's it—our primary job is done. The final step is to see the TradePersistor class in action to persist the trades to the database. This class delegates the persistence mechanism to TradeDAO.

See the following snippet:

```
public class TradePersistorUsingDAO {
  private ApplicationContext ctx = null;
  private TradeDAO tradeDAO = null;

  public TradePersistorUsingDAO() {
    ctx = new ClassPathXmlApplicationContext("hibernate-beans.xml");
    tradeDAO = ctx.getBean("tradeDAO",TradeDAO.class);
  }

  private void persist(Trade t) {
    tradeDAO.persist(t);
    System.out.println("Trade persisted:"+t);
  }

  public static void main(String[] args) {
    TradePersistorUsingDAO persistor = new TradePersistorUsingDAO();
    persistor.persist(DomainUtil.createDummyTrade());
  }
}
```

The class fetches a TradeDAO object reference from the Spring's container and calls the persist method on it by passing a Trade object. The job of actually persisting the Trade is taken care of by the TradeDAO as expected. The TradeDAO's persist method is shown below:

```
public class TradeDAO {
  ...
  public void persist(Trade t){
    // Obtain a session from the injected factory
    session = getSessionFactory().getCurrentSession();
    session.beginTransaction();
    session.save(t);
```

```
        session.getTransaction().commit();
        System.out.println("Trade successfully persisted");
    }
}
```

There are few interesting things going on in the above persist method. Before you start any data access operations using Hibernate's session, you must start a Transaction. You will learn about Transactions in detail shortly. For now, think of Transaction as a unit of work that either should succeed or fail. In the above case, the Trade object should either be persisted (Transaction is successful) or not persisted (Transaction is not successful). You cannot have only half the values of the Trade object written—you need to write the other half, too!

Once you begin your Transaction, the next step is to use Hibernate's Session API to do the data access. What we are doing is persisting the Trade by calling a save method on the session. The Trade will then be saved permanently in the database once the current transaction is committed, thus completing the unit of work.

The important point to note here is that you are using simple API calls to do the data access unlike the standard JDBC way. When you call the save method, for example, the object is transformed into the appropriate data row via your mapping file. This mapping is transparent to us, which is a great advantage. Working with Java objects instead of relational databases is a good thing in the object-oriented programming realm.

Because we will have to work with the transactions for every database call, it would be a good idea if we can wrap the start and commit transaction calls in a separate methods. The following code shows the respective methods that we should use in our code samples from now on:

```
// This method starts the transaction
private void beginTx() {
    session = getSessionFactory().getCurrentSession();
    session.beginTransaction();
}

// This method commits the current transaction
private void commitTx(){
    session.getTransaction().commit();
}
```

The above persist method can be simplified by removing the session transaction calls and using the above methods:

```
public void persist(Trade t){
    beginTx();
    session.save(t);
    commitTx();
    System.out.println("Trade successfully persisted");
}
```

Hibernate Operations

We have seen how to persist the `Trade` objects in our previous example. In this section, we will see a few examples using Hibernate's API. We will also go through the steps involved in manipulating the objects using Hibernate's powerful query support—Hibernate Query Language (HQL). HQL is similar to SQL, however it is more directed toward querying objects rather than data rows. For example, in order to fetch `trades` from our TRADES table, we write the query against our entity `Trade`. We do not expose database tables in the HQL constructs.

Finding a Single Row

Let's start with a simple example of finding a single `Trade` with a given `Trade id`. All we have to do is to create a query in the following form:

```
String query = "from Trade where id=:tradeId";
```

There are a couple of things to note from the above query. We query using the keyword *from* against our `Trade` POJO. The `where` clause is setting an `id` on the query, `id` being passed in via a method parameter. The last thing you notice is the assignment of the variable `id` (note that `Trade` has a variable defined as `id`). You use the colon (`:`) with a chosen name to set this `id`.

The next step is to create a Query object and set the relevant parameters to execute it:

```
public Trade getTrade(int tradeId) {
  String query = "from Trade where id=:tradeId";
  beginTx();
  Query q = session.createQuery(query)
    .setInteger("tradeId", 1);
  Trade t = (Trade) q.uniqueResult();
  commitTx();
  return t;
}
```

The `q.uniqueResult` will return a single `Trade` object from the TRADES table.

Finding Multiple Rows

The Hibernate's `Query` instance also supports returning a collection of objects. However, you do not have to instantiate the `Query` object as shown earlier—instead, invoke the `list()` method on it so you get the collection right away.

The following snippet demonstrates returning all `Trades` from the table:

```
public List<Trade> getAllTrades() {
  beginTx();
  List<Trade> trades = session.createQuery("from Trade").list();
  commitTx();
  return trades;
}
```

The *from Trade* is equivalent of saying to fetch all the **trades** from the table. So, appending the query with list() method returns you a collection as shown above.

Deleting Single Trade

In order to delete a single **trade** object, we have to use the delete method on the **session** object. The following code shows this:

```
public void delete(Trade t){
  beginTx();
  session.delete(t);
  commitTx();
}
```

It is simple if you know the row (or object) that you were going to delete.

Deleting Multiple Trades

We should use a query to delete muliple objects from the table. The following example shows such a query to delete all **trades** whose status is unknown.

```
public int deleteTradesByStatus(String status) {
  beginTx();

  String query = "delete from Trade where status = :status";

  // set the bind variables
  Query q = session.createQuery(query).setString("status",status)

  // the query execution results in rows affected
  int tradesDeleted = q.executeUpdate();

  commitTx();

  return tradesDeleted;
}
```

Spring's Job Is Done

In the last section, did you notice that we did not use the Spring framework when making the Hibernate calls? We used the framework only to inject the respective resources. As explained earlier, Spring's job more or less is done once the task of instantiating and injecting the appropriate objects, including the **SessionFactory**, is completed.

Spring really encourages us to use the Hibernate API to invoke any database operations. As this book is about Spring's support, unfortunately we cannot cover the Hibernate API in detail. I would strongly encourage you to pick up any good book on Hibernate to continue your journey.

However, should you use older versions of Spring (perhaps version 2.x), you could use the HibernateTemplate class, which follows the exact same principle as JbdcTemplate, seen in our first chapter.

Using HibernateTemplate

The HibernateTemplate wraps the Hibernate's Session method calls. It requires a SessionFactory to start with. As we have already defined a SessionFactory in our earlier examples, let's see how we create a HibernateTemplate.

We can create the class using pure configuration as shown below:

```
<bean id="hibernateTemplate"
class="org.springframework.orm.hibernate3.HibernateTemplate">
  <property name="sessionFactory" ref="sessionFactory"/>
</bean>

<bean id="sessionFactory"
  class="org.springframework.orm.hibernate3.LocalSessionFactoryBean">
  ....
</bean>
```

Alternatively, you could have an instance variable defined in your DAO:

```
//The SessionFactory is an injected instance
private SessionFactory sessionFactory = ...

// Create a new instance of HibernateTemplate with
// the injected SessionFactory
hibernateTemplate = new HibernateTemplate(sessionFactory);
```

After you have configured and instantiated the HibernateTemplate, you could invoke the appropriate data access methods. The following snippet shows a few of these invocations:

```
//Inserting a new trade

public void insertTrade(Trade t){
  template.save(t);
  System.out.println("Trade inserted using HibernateTemplate");
}

// Deleting a single trade
public void deleteTrade(Trade t){
  template.delete(t);
  System.out.println("Trade deleted using HibernateTemplate");
}

// Finding all trades for a given status
public void findAllTrades(String status){
  String tradeQuery = "from Trade t where status=?";
  List<Trade> trades = template.find(tradeQuery,status);
  System.out.println("Trade retrieved using HibernateTemplate:"+trades);
}
```

Should you require a `Session` instance to call some custom calls, you use the callback mechanism as shown below:

```
// Executing in a callback that returns a Session to you
public void inCallBack() {
  template.execute(new HibernateCallback(){

  @Override
  public Object doInHibernate(Session session)
    throws HibernateException, SQLException {
    // Use the session to execute custom calls
    ....
    return ..;
  }});
}
```

Hibernate Support Classes

Spring provides a `HibernateDaoSupport` class that lets you grab the `Session` and `HibernateTemplate` without having to worry about callbacks. You have to extend this class and set a `SessionFactory` as a mandatory requirement. See below for an example:

```
public class TradeHibernateSupportDAO extends HibernateDaoSupport {

  // Set the SessionFactory first
  public TradeHibernateSupportDAO(SessionFactory sessionFactory) {
    setSessionFactory(sessionFactory);
  }

  // Use the super class's methods
  public List<Trade> getAllTrades() {
    Session session = getSession(false);
    List<Trade> trades = session.createQuery("from Trade").list();
    return trades;
  }
}
```

Transactions

The Spring framework provides excellent support for `Transactions`. You can use annotations to achieve this goal or use the framework's Aspect Oriented Programming (AOP) techniques. We use annotations to demonstrate the usage here.

Declaring via annotations is by far the easy way.

First, annotate the respective class (usually your DAO) or its methods via the @Transactional annotation. This is shown below:

```
@Transactional
public class PriceDAO {
  ...
}
```

The above snippet makes *all* of the methods in the `PriceDAO` object work in `Transactional` mode. If you wish to have more granularity, then use the same annotation at the method level. This is shown below:

```
public class PriceDAO {
  ...
  @Transactional
  public void persist(Price p) {
    ..
  }

  @Transactional
  public void delete(Price p) {
    ..
  }
}
```

Once you have the `transactions` marked on your classes or methods, the next step is to wire in a `TransactionManager` bean. Spring provides different managers for various providers: `HibernateTrasactionManager` for Hibernate, `JpaTransactionManager` for JPA, `JdoTransactionManager` for JDO, and others.

We create a `HibernateTransactionManager` with a reference to `SessionFactory`, as illustrated below:

```
<bean id="transactionManager"
  class="org.springframework.orm.hibernate3.HibernateTransactionManager">
  <property name="sessionFactory" ref="sessionFactory" />
</bean>

<bean id="sessionFactory"
  class="org.springframework.orm.hibernate3.LocalSessionFactoryBean">
  ...
</bean>

<bean id="priceDAO" class="com.madhusudhan.jsd.hibernate.tx.PriceDAO">
  <property name="sessionFactory" ref="sessionFactory" />
</bean>
```

We also have to make sure that the annotated classes are picked up by the Spring runtime. This is done by adding the following line in the config file:

```
<beans xmlns="http://www.springframework.org/schema/beans"
  xmlns:xsi="http://www.w3.org/2001/XMLSchema-instance"
  xmlns:tx="http://www.springframework.org/schema/tx"
  xsi:schemaLocation="http://www.springframework.org/schema/beans
    http://www.springframework.org/schema/beans/spring-beans.xsd
    http://www.springframework.org/schema/tx
    http://www.springframework.org/schema/tx/spring-tx.xsd
    ...
    http://www.springframework.org/schema/context/spring-context-3.0.xsd">
```

```
<tx:annotation-driven transaction-manager="transactionManager"/>

...

</beans>
```

As shown above, don't forget to add the `tx` namespace, which is used to declare the annotation-driven element.

Ideally, you do not have to provide the `transaction-manager` attribute if the name of the `TransactionManager` is `transactionManager` as it is picked up as a default name. If however, you have a different name (say, `txManager`), you should indicate that by declaring the name using the `transaction-manager` attribute.

Summary

We initiated this chapter with an intention of learning the Object Relational Mapping (ORM) technology and its incompatability with the Java Object Model. In this chapter, we discussed Spring's support for the Hibernate framework. We breezed through the Hibernate basics and discussed Spring's basic setup for Hibernate in detail. We looked at the case of using plain Hibernate API using Spring's dependency injection mechanisms against the legacy `HibernateTemplate`'s mode. We also looked at Spring's help via `HibernateDaoSupport` class. We wrapped up the chapter by looking at enabling declarative `Transactions`.

CHAPTER 4

Spring JPA

When comes to ORM frameworks, plenty of frameworks exist. We have already seen Hibernate in our last chapter. Frameworks may have a free hand when it comes to implementation if no standard is around. A standard or a specification helps the end user in swapping the frameworks without much hassle should the need arise. Java folks realised the need of a persistence standard that would help the user community. The standard is called a Java Persistence API (JPA)—an API that helps to standardize the Java Persistence world.

In this chapter, we will look at the Java Persistence API at a high level and at Spring's support to use the API with few providers, especially with the Hibernate provider. As expected, there will be a few players who implement the specification and bring the standard to life. We see discuss one such provider—Hibernate itself—in this chapter.

Two-Minute JPA

The JPA defines an `EntityManager` interface, which is basically the heart of the API. It is similar to Hibernate's `Session`, forming the core of the application to perform database operations.

As you create `Session` from a `SessionFactory`, it's not hard to understand that you use `EntityManagerFactory` to create an instance of `EntityManager`. However, because JPA is a standard applicable to Enterprise and Standalone applications, there are a couple of modes for obtaining or creating the `EntityManagerFactory` itself—one that will be created in a managed environment such as Application Servers or Web containers while the other in a standalone application.

Once you have the `EntityManager` (obtained from `EntityManagerFactory`), the next step is to declare a *persistence unit*. A persistence unit is a logical group of persistent classes (called entities in JPA lingo), database settings, and relational mappings.

We will see the `EntityManager` and its factory in action in a few pages, but for now, let's look at the following snippet that indicates a `persistence-unit`:

```xml
<persistence xmlns="http://java.sun.com/xml/ns/persistence"
  xmlns:xsi="http://www.w3.org/2001/XMLSchema-instance"
  xsi:schemaLocation="http://java.sun.com/xml/ns/persistence
  http://java.sun.com/xml/ns/persistence/persistence_2_0.xsd"
  version="2.0">

  <persistence-unit name="trade-mysql-pu" transaction-type="RESOURCE_LOCAL">
    <provider>org.hibernate.ejb.HibernatePersistence</provider>
    <class>com.madhusudhan.jsd.domain.jpa.Trade</class>
    <properties>
      <property name="hibernate.connection.url"
        value="jdbc:mysql://localhost:3306/JSDATA"/>
      <property name="hibernate.connection.driver_class"
        value="com.mysql.jdbc.Driver"/>
      <property name="hibernate.dialect"
        value="org.hibernate.dialect.MySQL5Dialect"/>
      ...
    </properties>
  </persistence-unit>
</persistence>
```

As you can see, a `persistent-unit` named `trade-mysql-pu` was created with a single persistent entity (`Trade`) and the `HibernatePersistence` as the provider (the implementor of the JPA Specification). The properties indicate the settings of the database which are similar to the DataSource definition properties.

One norm you should follow is to create the `persistence.xml` file under a folder named `META-INF`. The providers are required to look for this file under that folder. If the folder doesn't exist, create one and add it to the classpath.

The class attribute defines the *persistent entity* as seen in the above XML file. We create an entity with appropriate annotations (`@Entity`, `@Column`, `@Id`, and so on).

See below for an example of how the `Trade` entity is defined:

```java
@Entity
@Table(name="TRADES")
public class Trade {
  @Column( nullable=false)
  @Id
  @GeneratedValue(strategy=GenerationType.AUTO)
  private int id = 0;

  @Column
  private String direction = null;

  @Column
  private String account = null;

  ...
```

The entity annotation describes that this POJO is a persistable entity (a domain object) which maps to the `TRADES` table. You do not have to provide the table details if the class name matches to the table name (in our case, the domain object is `Trade` which doesn't match to table TRADES). The properties follow the same path—they match to the column names.

The last thing to understand, which is covered in the next few pages, is how EntityManagerFactory's and EntityManager's are created.

The JPA specification classifies two types of entity managers: one that runs in a container-managed environment, and another that runs in a standalone JVM. The former one is typically a Java Enterprise Edition (JEE) container such as an application server or a web container, while the latter is a Java Standard Edition standalone program.

The EntityManager itself is no different in both types but the EntityManagerFactory that creates the EntityManager is a bit unique in how it is configured and created.

In a standalone environment, you should create the EntityManager as shown here:

```
private EntityManagerFactory factory = null;
private EntityManager entityManager = null;
..
private void init() {
  factory = Persistence.createEntityManagerFactory("trade-mysql-pu");
  entityManager = factory.createEntityManager();
}
```

You should pass in the name of the previously defined persistence unit (from persistence.xml) to the createEntityManagerFactory() method. We then obtain the EntityManager by calling createEntityManager on the factory.

In a container-managed environment, the class with a reference to the entity manager (typically DAO objects) will be injected with an existing EntityManager. The responsibility of looking up the persistence unit, creating the factory, and subsequently creating and injecting the EntityManager are all taken care of by the JEE application container.

Note that, however you get the EntityManager, whether from a JEE container or in a standalone mode, the operations on it are always the same. The fundamental difference involves its creation—not its workings.

Using Spring

What's the value input from Spring in supporting JPA, you might ask?

The Spring framework supports the JPA API in couple of ways, very similar to support for Hibernate. One way is by providing the classic template: a JpaTemplate class. This class is basically a wrapper around the EntityManager similar to other templates such as HibernateTemplate.

The second way is by allowing the developer to use plain JPA API in the applications via an injected EntityManager class. If you are confused as to what approach to take, go with using plain API if possible. This way, Spring will be used solely for dependency injection thus avoiding any dependencies on its framework classes. Should you have earlier versions (before 3.x), perhaps sticking to template style might be easier.

Let's explore both of these use cases in detail.

Basically, Spring encapsulates the EntityManagerFactory in its own FactoryBean implementation and injects them into the applications where it is needed.

Spring uses two implementations of FactoryBean for providing the EntityManagers in respective environments:

org.springframework.orm.jpa.LocalEntityManagerFactoryBean
    This FactoryBean creates the EntityManagerFactory for standalone environments. This implementation provides a simple factory that has limitations. It cannot participate in global transactions, cannot work with DataSources.

org.springframework.orm.jpa.LocalContainerEntityManagerFactoryBean
    This factory bean provides the EntityManagerFactory for enterprise environments. Note how its classname has the word "Container" embedded in it, compared to the previous LocalEntityManagerFactoryBean class.

We will see both of them in action in the next section.

Standalone Factory

In order to provide the EntityManager to your standalone Spring application, what we need to do is to define the LocalEntityManagerFactoryBean in your configuration file, as shown in the following snippet:

```
<bean id="entityManagerFactory"
  class="org.springframework.orm.jpa.LocalEntityManagerFactoryBean">
    <property name="persistenceUnitName" value="trade-mysql-pu" />
</bean>
```

Note that the persistenceUnitName refers to the persitence-unit name provided in the persistence.xml file. The bean is now configured and ready to be injected. The following snippet shows how it has been injected into our TradeDAO object:

```
<bean id="entityManagerFactory" ..

<bean id="tradeDAO" class="com.madhusudhan.jsd.jpa.TradeDAO">
    <property name="entityManagerFactory" ref="entityManagerFactory" />
</bean>
```

As expected, the factory will be injected into TradeDAO and it's the TradeDAO's job to create the EntityManager from the factory. This is shown in the following snippet:

```
private EntityManagerFactory entityManagerFactory = null;
private EntityManager manager = null;

public TradeDAO() {
  manager = getEntityManagerFactory().createEntityManager();
}
```

```
//setters for EntityManagerFactory - will be injected by Spring
public void setEntityManagerFactory(EntityManagerFactory entityManagerFactory) {
  this.entityManagerFactory = entityManagerFactory;
}

public EntityManagerFactory getEntityManagerFactory() {
  return entityManagerFactory;
}
```

Now that we have created the EntityManager instance, our job is done. We can use its contract API to execute data access operations such as creating, finding, and deleting entities, as well as many more operations against a database.

I've created few methods on the TradeDAO shown below:

```
public class TradeDAO {

  private EntityManagerFactory entityManagerFactory = null;
  private EntityManager manager = null;

  void persist(Trade t){
    // persist the object
    getManager().persist(t);
  }

  public void delete(Trade t){
    // delete the row
    getManager().remove(t);
  }
  ...
}
```

In order to insert a Trade object, we use the persist() method exposed on the Entity Manager. Obviously, we need to start a transaction before we execute any data access operation and commit the transaction. Similarly, there are a few other methods such as merge, remove, and find to do relevant operations. Please refer to the standard API documentation for more details on using these methods beyond the examples shown here.

Container Factory

It is time to see how Spring provides a managed entity factory. In this situation, Spring acts as a container itself and all configuration is managed in its context file. As we learned earlier, the EntityManagerFactory is encapsulated by LocalContainerEntityManagerFactoryBean, which is recommended for most of the applications, including those meant to be used as standalone programs. This factory provides support for global and local transactions while utilizing the existing Data Source definitions.

Let's see how we create the EntityManagerFactory via the Spring container.

Configuring the Factory

The following snippet shows the configuration required for creating the factory:

```xml
<bean id="entityManagerFactory"
    class="org.springframework.orm.jpa.LocalContainerEntityManagerFactoryBean">

  <property name="dataSource" ref="mySqlDataSource" />
  <property name="packagesToScan" value="com.madhusudhan.jsd.jpa" />

  <property name="jpaVendorAdapter">
    <bean class="org.springframework.orm.jpa.vendor.HibernateJpaVendorAdapter">
    <property name="showSql" value="true" />
    <property name="generateDdl" value="true" />
    <property name="databasePlatform"
      value="org.hibernate.dialect.MySQL5Dialect" />
  </bean>
  </property>
</bean>

<bean id="transactionManager"
class="org.springframework.orm.jpa.JpaTransactionManager">
  <property name="entityManagerFactory" ref="entityManagerFactory" />
</bean>

<bean id="mySqlDataSource" class="org.apache.commons.dbcp.BasicDataSource">
  ...
</bean>
```

There are few interesting properties that deserve mentioning:

The `dataSource` property refers to the standard JDBC DataSource that is configured in the same XML file as we did before (shown as Apache Common's DBCP DataSource in the snippet).

- The factory class points to the framework's `LocalContainerEntityManagerFactory Bean` class.
- The `pacakagesToScan` attribute instructs the framework to browse through the relevant package (`com.madhusudhan.jsd.jpa` in this case) to find the persistent entities by looking at the `@Entity` annotations on the class.
- The `jpaVendorAdapter` attributes tells the bean to use Hibernate's persistence provider. You may provide additional properties to the adapter such as `generateDdl`, `databasePlatform` (Dialect), `batchSize`, and so on.

Now that all the moving pieces are, or have been assembled, invoke the data access methods on `TradeDAO`. Because of all the changes we made previously were config related, there wouldn't be any changes to the DAO object. Hence you can re-use the same `TradeDAO`:

```java
public class TradeDAO {
  ...
  public void persist(Trade t){
    // persist the object
```

```
    getManager().persist(t);
  }

  public void delete(Trade t){
    // delete the row
    getManager().remove(t);
  }
  ...
}
```

Use the DAO to execute relevant data access functions. Inserting a new Trade would be extraordinarily simple, as demonstrated here:

```
public class TradePersistorTest {
  ...
  public TradePersistorTest() {
    ctx = new ClassPathXmlApplicationContext("jpa-beans.xml");
    dao = ctx.getBean("tradeDao",TradeDAO.class);
  }
  public void persist(Trade p){
    dao.persist(p);
  }

  public static void main(String[] args) {
    TradePersistorTest test = new TradePersistorTest();
    Trade t = new Trade();
    //..set values on Trade t
    test.persist(t);
  }
}
```

As you can see, once you get the DAO bean from the container, invoke the persist operation to store a new Trade.

Transactions

The above methods must be executed in a transaction. If you are using programmatic demarcation of transactions, perhaps each of your data access operation should begin with a new transaction and end the transaction when done. Of course, you can span your transaction across multiple operations.

The EntityManager exposes methods to begin, commit, and/or rollback transactions. For example, the following snippet shows utility methods that create a new transaction and commit an existing transaction:

```
//beginning your transaction
private void begin() {
  getManager().getTransaction().begin();
}

//committing your transaction
private void commit() {
  getManager().getTransaction().commit();
}
```

In our DAO, we should demarcate the `transactional` boundaries as shown below:

```
public void persist(Trade p){

    // begin your tx
    begin(); //calls the above begin method

    // do your job
    dao.persist(p);

    // end your transaction
    commit();// calls the above commit method
}
```

Spring also provides declarative transactional support. Please refer to section on declarative `transactions` discussed in Chapter 3.

Using Plain JPA API

While we can mix and match the framework's elements into our data access layer, the recommended approach is to use the plain JPA API to execute data access operations. Spring's support is excellent in achieving this goal, as we will see in few minutes.

The DAO's `setEntityManagerFactory` method should be annotated with `@PersistenceUnit` annotation. Spring understands this annotation and accordingly will inject `EntityManagerFactory` into the DAO.

See the reworked example DAO using `@PersistenceUnit` annotation:

```
public class TradeDAO {

  @PersistenceUnit
  public void setEntityManagerFactory
      (EntityManagerFactory entityManagerFactory)
  {
    this.entityManagerFactory = entityManagerFactory;
  }
  ...
}
```

Did you notice that there are no Spring classes in the above DAO? The `@PersistenceUnit` annotation belongs to the JPA specification, which makes our DAO fully JPA-compliant. However, how does Spring know that it has to inject an `EntityMa nagerFactory` when the method is annotated with `@PersistenceUnit` annotation?

Well, it turns out that the magic is performed by Spring's post processor bean: `PersistenceAnnotationBeanPostProcessor`. This bean is wired into your configuration XML, as shown below:

```
<!-- Reads the annotations -->
<bean

class="org.springframework.orm.jpa.support.PersistenceAnnotationBeanPostProcessor" />
```

```xml
<bean id="tradeDao" class="com.madhusudhan.jpa.plain.TradeDAO"/>

<bean id="entityManagerFactory"
  class="org.springframework.orm.jpa.LocalEntityManagerFactoryBean">

  <property name="persistenceUnitName" value="trade-mysql-pu" />
</bean>
```

The rest of the beans in the XML configuration file are self-explanatory. If you wish to eliminate declaring individual post processors as shown above, you can use the following snippet that scans all of the post processors:

```xml
<context:annotation-config/>
```

Now that you have all the ammunition you need, all you have to do is to execute the functionality on the DAO via your test classes.

```java
public class TradePersistorPlainJpaTest {

  public TradePersistorPlainJpaTest() {

    ctx = new ClassPathXmlApplicationContext("jpa-plain-beans.xml");

    dao = ctx.getBean("tradeDao",TradeDAO.class);
  }

  public void persist(Trade p){
    dao.persist(p);
  }
  ...
}
```

That's about it!

We explore the Spring's template support in the next section.

Using JpaTemplate

The JpaTemplate follows the same template pattern that we have observed all along in the Spring's framework. It encapsulates the nitty-gritty of EntityManager and EntityManagerFactory implementations.

 The JpaTemplate has been deprecated since Spring version 3.1.x. It is strongly advised to use JPA API rather than JpaTemplate if you are using or migrating to version 3.1.x.

Define a bean named jpaTemplate and wire it with an EntityManagerFactory. This is shown below:

```xml
<bean id="jpaTemplate" class="org.springframework.orm.jpa.JpaTemplate">
  <property name="entityManagerFactory" ref="entityManagerFactory" />
</bean>
```

Note that the `entityManagerFactory` is created from the pre-defined `persistence-unit` (unlike `ContainerManagerFactory` where the persistence unit definition is not required).

You do not need to change your definition of DAO.

Both are shown in the following snippet:

```xml
<!-- Using JPATemplate -->
<bean id="entityManagerFactory"
  class="org.springframework.orm.jpa.LocalEntityManagerFactoryBean">
    <property name="persistenceUnitName" value="trade-mysql-pu" />
</bean>

<bean id="tradeDao" class="com.madhusudhan.jpa.TradeDAO">
    <property name="entityManagerFactory" ref="entityManagerFactory" />
</bean>

<bean id="jpaTemplate".../>
```

The `TradeDAO` is :

```java
public class TradeDAO {
  private JpaTemplate jpaTemplate = null;

  public void persist(Trade t){
    getJpaTemplate().persist(t);
  }

  //setter and getter for jpaTemplate
  ...
}
```

Now that you have the DAO, fetch it via your application context and invoke the appropriate methods.

```java
public class TradePersistorJpaTemplateTest {

  public TradePersistorJpaTemplateTest() {
    ctx = new ClassPathXmlApplicationContext("jpa-beans.xml");
    dao = ctx.getBean("tradeDao",TradeDAO.class);
  }

  public void persist(Trade p){
    dao.persist(p);
  }
  ...
}
```

Note that `JpaTemplate` introduces another layer on top of your DAO layer, which is not really necessary.

Support Classes

As usual, Spring provides its *XXXSupport* classes for our convenience. All you have to do is to let your DAO class extend the framework's `JpaDaoSupport` class. It then will have a reference to `JpaTemplate`.

The DAO class should look like this:

```
public class JPAPriceDAOSupport extends JpaDaoSupport {
  public void persist(Trade t) {
    getJpaTemplate().persist(t);
  }
}
```

Because you have extended the `JpaDaoSupport` class, the `JpaTemplate` will be readily available to your DAO instance. As you can see, the `getJpaTemplate()` will return the template object which is then used to invoke the appropriate data access operations.

The wiring of the DAO bean is shown below, which gets a `EntityManagerFactory` instance:

```
<bean id="jpaPriceDAOSupport"
class="com.madhusudhan.jsd.jpa.support.JPAPriceDAOSupport">
  <property name="entityManagerFactory" ref="entityManagerFactory" />
</bean>

<bean id="entityManagerFactory"
  class="org.springframework.orm.jpa.LocalEntityManagerFactoryBean">
    <property name="persistenceUnitName" value="TradePU" />
</bean>
```

Internally, the support class relies on `JpaTemplate` to do the actual work.

Note that the `JpaDaoSupport` class is deprecated in Spring version 3.1 or later. This way, Spring folks strongly encourage you to move on to using Spring with plain JPA API.

Summary

In this chapter, we looked at the Java Persistence API (JPA) from a very high level. We then tried to understand the Spring's support in bringing the JPA into our Java application world. We learned about the `EntityManagerFactory` and `EntityManager` which form the basis to understanding the JPA solutions. We also looked at standalone versus managed environments, and ways to create the factories and instantiate the `EntityMan agers` in these environments. We created our examples using plain JPA API and framework-dependent templates and support classes.

CHAPTER 5

Spring JDO

Java Data Objects (JDO) is yet another Java standard for persisting the Java POJOs. We have already seen JPA in Chapter 4. This chapter concentrates on JDO aspects of data access, how the Spring framework helps in configuring and using JDO in our Java applications. While JPA mainly works against relational databases, JDO is database-agnostic. You can think of any type of data stores such as object databases, NoSQL data stores, filesystems, email, XML, and so on.

In this chapter, we will look at the primary interfaces that JDO specification defines and how Spring provides support for using JDO-compliant providers in our Java application. As expected, the Spring framework is mainly used for dependency injection.

Spring Support

If you have been through the previous chapter on JPA, this chapter won't come as a surprise.

Similar to `EntityManagerFactory` in JPA, there's a factory class in JDO as well: `PersistenceManagerFactory`. Just as `EntityManager` was the core of JPA, `PersistenceManager` is used similarly within the JDO world. Use the factory object to fetch your `Persistence Manager` and accordingly invoke the relevant data access operations.

Spring can help your application development in a couple of ways. You can either work with a standard `JdoTemplate` or use a plain JDO API.

While Spring provides the convenient `JdoTemplate`, the preferred way of doing things since Spring version 3 is to use the native APIs while allowing Spring to inject the necessary factories.

So let's start understanding this usage right away.

As always, there will be both commercial and open source providers implementing the standard specifications. The DataNucleus (http://www.datanucleus.org) is one example of open source JDO implementors. We will be using this implementation for our examples, but it shouldn't be difficult to swap with other providers. That's the beauty of sticking to standards—you can switch to any providers at your own wish!

Let's see the steps involved in preparing our application with JDO using Spring framework. We discuss the steps for using JDO API via the Spring framework first.

Plain JDO API

Spring will help to inject the relevant factories into our applications so you have a handle of `PersistenceManager` instance. Once you have this handle, use the contract methods to persist or update the entities.

We need a POJO entity which is designed to be persistent, a DAO class to persist this entity, and a configuration XML file that defines the wiring of the beans. Note that JDO specification uses annotations as a method of declaring the persistent entities.

In JDO, there's also an additional step of enhancing your classes using byte code enhancers, which we'll see in a minute.

Persistent Entity

The POJO object that represents your persistent entity should be annotated with `@PersistenceCapable` annotation. The fields that are persistent should be annotated with `@Persistent` annotation.

The following shows the `JDOPrice` annotated in this way:

```
@PersistenceCapable(table = "PRICE")
public class JDOPrice {

    @Persistent
    @PrimaryKey
    private int id = 0;

    @Persistent
    private String security = null;

    @Persistent
    private double price = 0.0;

    //getters and setters
    ...
}
```

The `@PrimaryKey` annotation represents that field (`id` in the above entity) as the primary key of the table. You can use different strategies of generating or setting the primary keys. You should use the `valueStrategy` parameter on the `@PrimaryKey` annotation. For example `IdGeneratorStrategy.IDENTITY` sets the database-generated `id` value as shown below:

```
@PersistenceCapable(table = "PRICE")
public class JDOPrice {
  @Persistent
  @PrimaryKey(valueStrategy=IdGeneratorStrategy.IDENTITY)
  private int id = 0;
```

Persistence DAO

The next piece of work is to create a DAO object that accomplishes the actual persistence. Obviously, it should be injected with a `PersistenceManagerFactory` instance.

```
public class JDOPriceDAO {

  private PersistenceManagerFactory persistenceManagerFactory = null;

  public void setPersistenceManagerFactory(PersistenceManagerFactory
persistenceManagerFactory) {
    this.persistenceManagerFactory = persistenceManagerFactory;
  }

  public PersistenceManagerFactory getPersistenceManagerFactory() {
    return persistenceManagerFactory;
  }

  // Use the PM to persist our Price object
  public void persist(JDOPrice p){
    getPersistenceManagerFactory().getPersistenceManager().makePersistent(p);
    System.out.println("Persisted:"+p);
  }
}
```

The factory is then used to create a `PersistenceManager` that is used to access your data store and invoke relevant data access operations.

Wiring the Pieces

The configuration and wiring of these beans along with the DAO are provided in jdo-beans.xml, which is shown below:

```
<bean id="persistenceManagerFactory"
class="org.datanucleus.api.jdo.JDOPersistenceManagerFactory">
  <property name="connectionFactory" ref="mySqlDataSource" />
</bean>

<bean id="mySqlDataSource" class="org.apache.commons.dbcp.BasicDataSource">
  //..
</bean>

<bean id="priceDao" class="com.madhusudhan.jsd.jdo.JDOPriceDAO">
  <property name="persistenceManagerFactory"
    ref="persistenceManagerFactory" />
</bean>
```

An instance of `DataSource` should be provided to the `PersistenceManagerFactory`. Note that we are using DataNucleus's implementation for the JDO specification, hence the factory points to the DataNucleus's `JDOPersistenceManagerFactory` implementation class.

Now that you have all the pieces in hand, executing a test is simple, as shown below:

```
public class JDOTest {
  ...
  public JDOTest() {
    ctx = new ClassPathXmlApplicationContext("jdo-beans.xml");
    priceDAO = ctx.getBean("priceDao", JDOPriceDAO.class);
  }
  // use the DAO object to persist the Price
  private void persist(JDOPrice p) {
    priceDAO.persist(p);
  }

  public static void main(String[] args) {
    JDOTest test = new JDOTest();
    JDOPrice p = ...
    test.persist(p);
  }
}
```

The `persist()` call is delegated to the DAO, while the DAO calls the `makePersistent()` method on the `PersistenceManager` to persist the DAO. It is straight forward to invoke any operations exposed by the `PersistenceManager` once you have an instance available from the factory.

Before you can start executing the tests, one step remains: manipulating your generated classes so they implement the mandatory interfaces. This is carried out by a process called bytecode enhancement, which is detailed in next section.

Bytecode Enhancers

Bytecode enhancement is a post-compilation step to be carried out on the persistent entities. Basically, this step takes the generated POJO entity class file and enhances it to implement the `PersistenceCapable` (remember that the entity we defined has an `@PersistenceCapable` annotation) interface.

DataNucleus uses its own enhancement mechanisms to do this job. All you have to do is execute the following command against the generated classes:

```
export CLASSPATH=target/classes
  :lib/datanucleus-enhancer-3.0.1.jar
  :lib/datanucleus-core-3.0.10.jar
  :lib/datanucleus-api-jdo-3.0.7.jar
  :lib/jdo-api-3.1-SNAPSHOT-20110926.jar
  :lib/asm-3.3.jar

java -cp
```

```
target/classes:$CLASSPATH org.datanucleus.enhancer.DataNucleusEnhancer
target/classes/com/madhusudhan/jsd/jdo/*.class
```

Set your classpath with the required DataNucleus libraries and pass your generated classes to the `DataNucleusEnhancer` class. The `DataNucleusEnhancer` will then manipulate the .class files (bytecode) and produces appropriate classes.

Obviously a command line utility is no good when you have a continuous integration or sophisticated build in place. DataNucleus provides two more options to carry out bytecode enhancements in addition to the command line method: using Ant or Maven plugin. Refer to their documentation for more details on how to use Ant or Maven to utilize enhancers.

Example Test

Now that you have all the pieces in hand, executing a test is simple, as shown below:

```
public class JDOTest {
  ...
  public JDOTest() {
    ctx = new ClassPathXmlApplicationContext("jdo-beans.xml");
    priceDAO = ctx.getBean("priceDao", JDOPriceDAO.class);
  }
  // use the DAO object to persist the Price
  private void persist(JDOPrice p) {
    priceDAO.persist(p);
  }

  public static void main(String[] args) {
    JDOTest test = new JDOTest();
    JDOPrice p = ...
    test.persist(p);
  }
}
```

The `persist()` call is delegated to the DAO, while the DAO calls the `makePersistent()` method on the `PersistenceManager` to persist the DAO. It is straight forward to invoke any operations exposed by the `PersistenceManager` once you have an instance available from the factory.

As mentioned earlier, it is a good practice to stick to native APIs and code rather than inducing unnecessary Spring dependencies.

However, should you wish to use Spring's classic templates, the next section is for you.

Working with JdoTemplate

Working with `JdoTemplate` couldn't be any simpler, thanks to Spring's standard template designs.

The `JdoTemplate` is constructed by passing an instance of `PersistenceManagerFactory` —we have already seen setting up the factory bean earlier.

We need to create is a DAO that instantiates the JdoTemplate using the factory reference.

The JdoTemplate instance is created as such:

```java
public class JdoTemplatePriceDAO {
  private PersistenceManagerFactory persistenceManagerFactory = null;
  private JdoTemplate jdoTemplate = null;

  public void setPersistenceManagerFactory
    (PersistenceManagerFactory persistenceManagerFactory) {
    jdoTemplate = new JdoTemplate(persistenceManagerFactory);
  }

  public PersistenceManagerFactory getPersistenceManagerFactory() {
    return persistenceManagerFactory;
  }
}
```

Now that you have a handle on creating a JdoTemplate instance, you can use the instance to execute the required data access operations:

```java
public class JdoTemplatePriceDAO {
  // persisting singe price
  public void persist(JDOPrice p){
    jdoTemplate.makePersistent(p);
  }

  //persisting list of prices
  public void persistAllPrices(List<JDOPrice> prices){
    jdoTemplate.makePersistentAll(prices);
  }
  ...
}
```

Lastly, wire all the beans as shown below:

```xml
<bean id="persistenceManagerFactory"
class="org.datanucleus.api.jdo.JDOPersistenceManagerFactory">
  <property name="connectionFactory" ref="mySqlDataSource" />
</bean>

<bean id="jdoTemplatePriceDAO"
class="com.madhusudhan.jsd.jdo.template.JdoTemplatePriceDAO">
  <property name="persistenceManagerFactory" ref="persistenceManagerFactory" />
</bean>

<bean id="mySqlDataSource" ..</bean>
```

You can also create the JdoTemplate in the configuration and inject it into your DAO bean rather than creating it in your code:

```xml
<bean id="jdoTemplatePriceDAO"
class="com.madhusudhan.jsd.jdo.template.JdoTemplatePriceDAO">
  <property name="jdoTemplate" ref="jdoTemplate" />
</bean>

<bean id="jdoTemplate" class="org.springframework.orm.jdo.JdoTemplate">
```

```
    <property name="persistenceManagerFactory"
      ref="persistenceManagerFactory" />
</bean>
```

This saves you from having to create the `JdoTemplate` instance in your code. Instead. it will be created during the container configuration and readily available to your DAO bean. Make sure you have setters and getters defined on the DAO so the property can be set on the bean:

```
public class JdoTemplatePriceDAO {
  private JdoTemplate jdoTemplate = null;

  public JdoTemplate getJdoTemplate() {
    return jdoTemplate;
  }

  public void setJdoTemplate(JdoTemplate jdoTemplate) {
    this.jdoTemplate = jdoTemplate;
  }
  ...
}
```

That's it—once you have the `JdoTemplate` instance available, you can invoke the relevant methods to carry out your data access jobs.

Note that `JdoTemplate` is deprecated in Spring version 3.1.x or later in order to encourage you to move on to using JDO with plain API.

Support Classes

There's another way of using Spring JDO.

As usual, Spring provides yet another option. Using its *Support* classes. In this case, we can extend our DAO with the framework's `JdoDaoSupport` class that will have a reference to `JdoTemplate`.

The DAO class will look like this:

```
public class JDOPriceDAOSupport extends JdoDaoSupport {

  public void persist(JDOPrice p){
    getJdoTemplate().makePersistent(p);
  }

}
```

The `JdoTemplate` will be readily available to the DAO class once you extend the `JdoDao Support` class. As you can see, the `getJdoTemplate()` returns the template object, which is then used to invoke the appropriate data access operations.

The wiring of the DAO bean is shown below, which gets a `PersistenceManagerFac tory` instance:

```
<bean id="jdoPriceDAOSupport"
class="com.madhusudhan.jsd.jdo.support.JDOPriceDAOSupport">
  <property name="persistenceManagerFactory" ref="persistenceManagerFactory" />
</bean>
```

Internally, the support class relies on `JdoTemplate` to do the actual work.

As mentioned earlier, it is advisable to work with the plain JDO API rather than any of the variants of the `JdoTemplate` (including `JdoDaoSupport`) classes.

Note that the `JdoDaoSupport` class is deprecated in Spring version 3.1.x or later. This way, the Spring folks encourage you to move on to using JDO with plain API.

JDO versus JPA versus Hibernate

One of the common questions that crosses our minds is deciding which persistence solution to use: JDO, JPA, or Hibernate. There are a number of articles and discussions online, at times involving parties mudslinging at one another.

When it comes to standards, JDO and JPA stand first. Unfortunately, there is no right or wrong answer as both JDO and JPA standards are equally good and fit the persistence bill. It is interesting to note that both of these standards were developed by the Java Community Process (JCP). The JDO was born during early 2000, while the JPA emerged out of Enterprise Java Bean (EJB) 3 specification.

I believe that one of these unfortunate developments occurred due to political reasons. As a result, these two standards were produced.

If you have a stronger requirement of swapping the RDBMS to other types databases (such as object databases, flat files, Excel spreadsheets, XML, and so on) in your project in the near future, perhaps JDO may be the better option. Having said that, JPA can be tweaked to perform against non-RDBMS if push comes to shove!

I would say JPA is more of an API addressing the ORM side of things, while JDO has a superset of features to cover more of a datastore-agnostic! If you have a database vendor lock-in or perhaps rely upon specific database extensions or features, then perhaps JPA might be the right path to choose as there's little to no chance of moving away from that vendor in near future.

Even though Hibernate has been the most popular open source ORM framework out there, it was not based on standards—at least not the native API implementation. Having said that, it has extended its support for JPA and now implements JPA spec too. It provides Hibernate JPA API alongside its native API.

You can choose the JPA-compliant Hibernate API as opposed to using Hibernate's native API if you are paranoid about vendor lock-ins!

Summary

We learned another mechanism of persisting the Java Data Objects in this chapter in detail and Spring's helpful hand in maintaining a dependency framework. We highlighted steps involved in preparing an application to use plain JDO API. We carried out our examples using one of the JDO specification providers: DataNucleus. We also saw the usage of classic `JdoTemplate`. Finally we engaged ourselves in understanding the different persistence solutions offered by JDO, JPA, and Hibernate.

About the Author

Madhusudhan Konda is an experienced Java consultant working in London, primarily with investment banks and financial organizations. Having worked in enterprise and core Java for the last 12 years, his interests lie in distributed, multi-threaded, n-tier scalable, and extensible architectures. He is experienced in designing and developing high-frequency and low-latency application architectures. He enjoys writing technical papers and is interested in mentoring.

Have it your way.

Get even more for your money.

Join the O'Reilly Community, and register the O'Reilly books you own. It's free, and you'll get:

- $4.99 ebook upgrade offer
- 40% upgrade offer on O'Reilly print books
- Membership discounts on books and events
- Free lifetime updates to ebooks and videos
- Multiple ebook formats, DRM FREE
- Participation in the O'Reilly community
- Newsletters
- Account management
- 100% Satisfaction Guarantee

Signing up is easy:

1. **Go to: oreilly.com/go/register**
2. **Create an O'Reilly login.**
3. **Provide your address.**
4. **Register your books.**

Note: English-language books only

To order books online:
oreilly.com/store

For questions about products or an order:
orders@oreilly.com

To sign up to get topic-specific email announcements and/or news about upcoming books, conferences, special offers, and new technologies:
elists@oreilly.com

For technical questions about book content:
booktech@oreilly.com

To submit new book proposals to our editors:
proposals@oreilly.com

O'Reilly books are available in multiple DRM-free ebook formats. For more information:
oreilly.com/ebooks

Spreading the knowledge of innovators   oreilly.com

Lightning Source UK Ltd.
Milton Keynes UK
UKHW032020191022
410751UK00010B/1360